Woodland Style

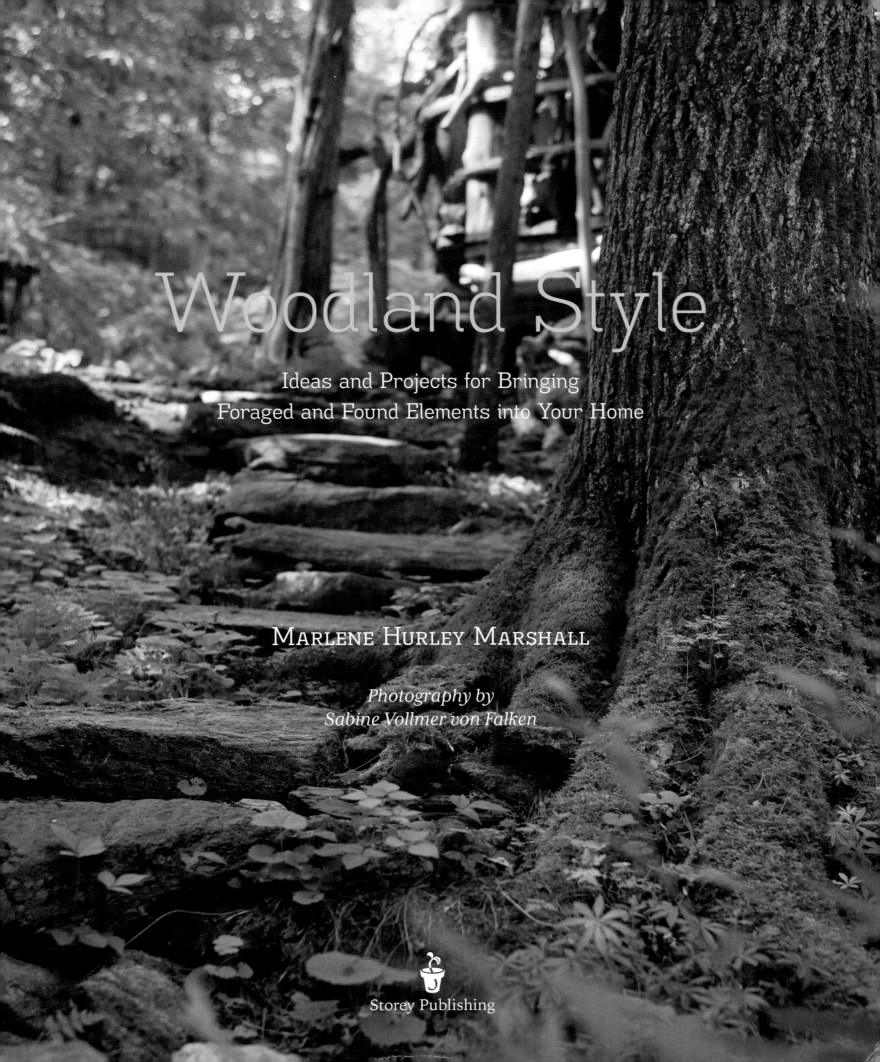

Woodland Style

Ideas and Projects for Bringing
Foraged and Found Elements into Your Home

MARLENE HURLEY MARSHALL

Photography by
Sabine Vollmer von Falken

Storey Publishing

*The mission of Storey Publishing is to serve our customers by
publishing practical information that encourages
personal independence in harmony with the environment.*

Edited by Deborah Balmuth and Cindy Littlefield
Art direction and book design by Alethea Morrison
Text production by Liseann Karandisecky

Photography by Sabine Vollmer von Falken,
    except as noted below
Photo styling by Marlene Hurley Marshall

Indexed by Catherine F. Goddard

Storey Publishing
210 MASS MoCA Way
North Adams, MA 01247
www.storey.com

Printed in China by R.R. Donnelley
10 9 8 7 6 5 4 3 2 1

Library of Congress Cataloging-in-Publication Data

Marshall, Marlene Hurley.
 Woodland style / by Marlene Hurley Marshall.
   p. cm.
 Includes index.
 ISBN 978-1-60342-552-0 (paper with flaps : alk. paper)
 1. Nature craft. I. Title.
TT157.M4185 2010
745.5—dc22
                    2010009717

ADDITIONAL PHOTO CREDITS
© Fritz Haeg: 125
© Linda B. Horn: 72 middle, 81
© Kevin Inkawhich: 40
© Connie Korbel: 38
The National Trust for Scotland: 8
© Susan Copen Oken: 36 bottom, 69, 150 bottom right
© Richard Reames/Arborsmith Studios: 86, 87
Christopher Simon Sykes © THE WORLD OF INTERIORS: 9
Faux Bois by © Donald R. Tucker, Houston, Texas: 152
Mars Vilaubi: 13 (except row 3 right center & right; row 4
    left center), 41, 68, 79, 124 bottom
© Roger Whiteway/iStockphoto.com: 124 top
© Tom Zetterstrom, from the Portrait of Trees series: 84, 85

Contents

Preface, 7

Introduction, 8

CHAPTER 1
Foraging for Materials, 11

CHAPTER 2
Twigs, Vines, and Roots, 19

CHAPTER 3
Pinecones, Acorns, and Seedpods, 47

CHAPTER 4
Moss, Greens, and Wildflowers, 59

CHAPTER 5
Trees, Logs, and Bark, 83

CHAPTER 6
Wild Edibles, 107

CHAPTER 7
Holiday and Seasonal Decorations, 127

CHAPTER 8
Stone and Faux Bois, 149

Resources and Credits, 156

Index, 159

To the branches of my family tree,
Michael, Leigh, Marlo, Quinn, Henry, and Amelia

Acknowledgments

My sincere thanks to all the creative artists who agreed to participate and made this book rich in creative ideas: Patrick Blanc, David Boag, Paul Busse, Sara Burke, Olena Bachinsky, Barbara Bockbrader, Luke and Bonnie Barrow, Anna Brahms, Carole Clark, Janet Cooper, Len Campanale, Jack DeMuth, Quinn Doherty, Henry Doherty, Patrick Dougherty, Sarah Dibben, Ivy Cote Fairbrother, Erica Fielder, Anne Fredericks, Ann Getsinger, Ellen Grenadier, Robin Greeson, Andy Goldsworthy, James Gottlieb, Pamela Hardcastle, Susie Hardcastle, Linda Horn, Kevin Inkawhich, Mimi Krysiak, Joan Meakin, Michael Melle, John Manikowski, Mariette Moon, Alex Malarkey, Don McAulay Jr., Tyler Moore, Nick Nickerson, Susie Oken, Nic Osborn, Gail Peachin, José Pimentel, Vicci Recckio, Richard Reames, Susie Schwartz, Joan Sussman, Donald Tucker, Sarah Thorne, Peter Thorne, Sabine Vollmer von Falken, Lisa Vollmer, and Tom Zetterstrom for branching out and taking a walk with me into the woods.

Special thanks to the many other people who made my project possible through their generosity in giving access to their interiors and exteriors: Robin Norris and Barbara Bockbrader from Campo de' Fiori; Brad Wagstaff and Leslie Miller from Gedney Farm and Peter Platt from the Old Inn On The Green, all from New Marlborough, Massachusetts; Lili and Loo, Madison Art & Antiques, Vince Mulford Antiques, Hudson Home, Keystone antique shop, Gottleib Gallery, and Olana State Historic Site, all of Hudson, New York; Dream Away Lodge in Becket, Massachusetts; Mrs. Charley Levine of Boston, Massachusetts; Luke and Bonnie Barrow from Rustic Garden Structures, Bynum, North Carolina; and the New York Botanical Garden, Bronx, New York.

Additional special thanks to David Rothstein, Allegra Graham, and Eve Zatt from Stagecoach Inn and Race Brook Tavern in Sheffield, Massachusetts, for hosting our Woodland Chic luncheon. Also to Susan Oken, who generously opened her Martha's Vineyard house and garden for several days of photography, and Elaine Rush, who invited us to photograph her extensive collection of woodland folk art in her Massachusetts home.

Big thanks to Deborah Balmuth, Cindy Littlefield, Alethea Morrison, Mars Vilaubi, and all the great staff at Storey Publishing for all their knowledge, hard work, and commitment to excellence.

Last, thanks to Mother Nature, who made our journey into the woods delightful.

Preface

WHEN I MOVED FROM THE CITY TO THE COUNTRY in 1978, the richness of the woodlands and the countryside surrounding my farmhouse filled me with awe. Where I grew up close to inner-city Boston, in the urban community of Charlestown, there were few trees or gardens. So here I was, a true city girl, living in a 200-year-old farmhouse on 17 acres in western Massachusetts. This was the beginning of my love affair with nature.

The house was a bit neglected, with overgrown lilacs and forsythia bushes, untended apple, pear, and cherry trees, and horseradish growing everywhere. There was a multitude of wild irises around the pond and chive flower heads as big as golf balls. Beyond the house were miles of bog inhabited in early April by chirping peepers. It was also the site of fallen trees, beaver dams, moss, marsh marigolds, and skunk cabbage. In the fall, I would look out the window to see Queen Anne's lace, golden-rod, wild asters, a variety of berries, and deer grazing on fallen fruit. Each season brought its own bouquet of wild materials to gather. I started gardening in those early days and have been an avid gardener ever since.

Today I live in the small city of Hudson, New York, where I have limited garden space, but that hasn't stopped me from creating a lush, wildly overplanted yard and enjoying walks in the woods. A few miles outside the city are acres of orchards, nature preserves, and the wonderful Hudson River. And having two choco-late Labrador retrievers ensures that my daily walks occur year-round no matter what the weather.

With my background as an artist, it didn't take me long to start creating art from objects I gathered during my walks in the woods. I had designed and created mosaics with bits of china and shells for many years, so using woodland elements was a perfect next step. Once I began this work, I discovered a rich history of other artists and craftspeople inspired by nature. I was fasci-nated by photographs from Europe of refined, sophisti-cated vintage mosaic work done with pinecones, acorns, heather, and bark. I could see so many new possibilities for the baskets I filled with natural materials gathered from the woods. And from that the idea for this book was born. My hope is that it will present the natural world in a new light that inspires the reader to recognize the beauty that exists in all seasons and to use nature's offer-ings in creative ways.

— MARLENE HURLEY MARSHALL

Introduction

Ever since ancient times, nature has been revered; the oldest sanctuaries were the natural woods themselves. The evergreen, for example, represented eternal life to the pagans. The Druids built temples in the woods and worshipped trees as the source of food, fuel, and shelter. The Tree of Life is a symbol that holds cultural and religious significance in nearly every society and is referred to in the Book of Genesis as "The Wood of Life."

At present, our culture is at a crossroads in its relationship with nature. We are increasingly aware of the negative impact human activity has on the environment and concerned about the future of natural resources. Many people are working hard to reconnect to the belief that nature is a force to be protected, respected, nurtured, and enjoyed. In a high-tech society, we're finding that increased contact with nature can have a calming and centering effect in our lives. A simple encounter with nature is a sparkling moment to be embraced and enjoyed.

With this book that celebrates the historic connection of nature to our culture and daily lives, I hope to encourage continuation of the tradition of using organic elements of nature in art, and to introduce arts and artists who shine a spotlight on nature's beauty and bounty. The projects featured on the following pages show just a small sampling of the vast array of natural materials that are accessible for our creative use, most of which are freely available in the woods, in the meadows, and, sometimes, right in our own backyards.

A Bavarian Summerhouse

One of the first inspirations for this book was an article that I read about Brodick Castle on the Isle of Arran in Scotland. Here, a summerhouse was built in the rustic

This starburst ceiling pattern crafted from hazel twigs and pinecones adorns the summer house at Brodick Castle.

Bavarian style in honor of the young Princess Marie of Baden, the daughter of the Grand Duke of Baden, who left her glittering court and moved to this remote island to wed William, the eleventh Duke of Hamilton. In 1845, a boatload of Bavarian craftsmen arrived to construct this hexagonal structure. Twisted branches and twigs were used to create trellis-style exterior walls and lattice-covered windows. Inside, the walls were lined with long pinecones and the ceiling was covered with scores of pinecones in all sizes, arranged in intricate patterns. And this impressive handiwork was done with natural elements found in the woods surrounding the grounds.

Heather Houses

Another early source of inspiration was learning about the rustic Victorian heather-clad summerhouses deep in the woods surrounding Drumlanrig Castle in Scotland. The ancient stronghold of the Montagu-Douglas-Scott family and the dukes of Buccleuch and Queensberry, Drumlanrig is the site of the first Douglas fir to be planted in Britain, the seeds having been sent over from North America in the early 1800s. The huts, known as the Heather Houses, were built and decorated by local artisans.

Each of these four Heather Houses is unique, but all incorporate the very Scottish product of dried heather. The interior walls are covered with it, and braided heather upholsters the benches. Even the roofs were originally covered with heather before being replaced with slate. Each Heather House reflects its own interpretation of the family's various coats of arms, with diamonds, crescents, and stars depicted on large interior panels.

Today, Drumlanrig is home to a conifer conservation project directed by the Earl of Dalkeith. A new species of rhododendron from China and the Himalayas grows there as well, and stonewalls built in the eighteenth century have been uncovered.

These stunning, large-scale examples of how people have created structures that bring the feeling and beauty of the woods into interior living spaces set the scene for my exploration of woodland style.

Different natural materials and techniques were used to achieve the effects on walls and ceilings in these two Heather Houses.
LEFT Silver birch embedded with braided heather; RIGHT Sphagnum moss soaked in lime wash, with silver birch twigs.

A Sampling of Moss and Bark

1 Hair cap moss (*Polytrichum* sp.)
2 Orthotrichum moss (*Orthotrichum anomalum*)
3 Broom moss (*Dicranum* sp.)
4 Hypnum moss (*Hypnum pallescens*)
5 Callicladium moss (*Callicladium haldanianum*)
6 Atrichum moss (*Atrichum angustatum*)

7 Dicranum moss (*Dicranum fulvum*)
8 Fire moss, a.k.a. Purple horned moss (*Ceratodon purpureus*)
9 Silver maple (*Acer saccharinum*)
10 Red maple (*Acer rubrum*)
11 River birch (*Betula nigra*)

12 White birch (*Betula papyrifera*)
13 White pine (*Pinus strobus*)
14 Lichen-covered sugar maple (*Acer saccharum*)
15 Cottonwood (*Populus freemonti*)
16 Black birch (*Betula lenta*)

ECO TIP

A permit to collect bark, pinecones, mushrooms, and other woodland materials in national and state parks usually can be obtained from the park management service (the USDA Forest Service, the National Park Service, the state forest department, or another local agency).

On a winter walk there is so much to discover. Here a lone weathered leaf was found resting on a bed of snow.

Handy Places to Collect Natural Materials

There are many practical and easy sources for acquiring crafting supplies. Before you head out to explore new places, take a look around your own backyard. There's a large weeping pine tree in my own yard, for example, that drops multitudes of pinecones. In addition, my neighbor has a weeping pine tree that hangs over my fence and sends down a few thousand more! And a friend offered me the bark from the pine trees she plans to remove from her yard. As part of spring cleanup, many homeowners clear fallen or pruned fruit tree branches that may still have buds. If so, you can take them indoors to force the blooms. You may also find places where local road crews are trimming trees in the downtown area or developers are clearing plots for new homes. Just be sure to ask permission before scavenging through the cuttings.

When to Collect What

Every season has its special features and limitations, but there is never a time when collecting natural objects is altogether impossible. In the northern region where I live, for example, spring brings certain varieties of wildflowers, such as violets and wild iris. Summer features daisies, wild roses, phlox, mullein, and other blooms and leaves in a wide variety of shapes, colors, and sizes. The fall is best for finding pods and collecting vibrantly colored leaves that are still moist and in near perfect condition. It's also the season for Queen Anne's lace, staghorn sumac, asters, and other late bloomers. From late fall through early spring is the ideal time for collecting vines that are supple and easy to work. And winter months are prime for collecting bark, twigs, stones, lichen, and year-round green moss. I have even found intact leaves under the snow.

Cleaning Collected Materials

When you bring newfound materials home, leave them outside for several days. This allows them to maintain moisture and provides time for any lingering bugs to detach. Insects are the biggest problem when collecting woodland materials. Another option is to put the materials in large garbage bags and then spray them with an insect spray or add cedar balls. Tie the bags closed and let them stand for a few days. In preparation for my Woodland Chic workshop at a local museum, each student was required to freeze any natural materials for 24 hours before using them in the workshop to guarantee that no pests would be brought into the building.

When You're in a Pinch

Remember, if you're decorating for a big event and time is limited, or if you're designing something that requires a large volume of twigs, acorns, birch bark, or moss, you can purchase many of these materials at a local craft store or online. Although you will miss out on the enjoyable process of discovering these materials in their natural habitat, the bonus is that they will already be clean.

Storing and Preserving Your Collection

The best place to store woodland finds depends on the specific materials. Those stored indoors should be properly ventilated so that they will dry without molding. The exception is grapevines and like materials that you want to be flexible. Either use them immediately or store them outside in the shade where they are more apt to maintain their moisture.

Bark

Store bark outside or in a shed, basement, or garage. Place it on a flat surface with a weight on top to keep it from curling up if you plan on hanging it on a wall or using it as a serving surface. Or use the curled shape bark naturally takes as part of a design. Let the bark dry completely and sweep it with a hand broom several times to make sure it is dust-free before using it.

Leaves

Collect leaves in the summer or fall when they are moist and pliable and often vibrantly colored. Lay them, not touching, between stacks of newspaper sheets or between magazine pages topped with a heavy book or other weight to keep them flat. For the first several days, turn the leaves over to check for mold, which can develop if they were too wet when collected. When collecting fall branches of leaves to display in a vase, do so just as the leaves begin to turn. They will be in their finest condition and, if placed in water, will maintain their vibrancy for about two weeks.

Pinecones, Acorns, and Pods

All of these natural elements can simply be stored in plastic containers once they are completely dry. Punching a few air holes through the plastic will help keep them ventilated and prevent mold. Storing each type of material in a separate container will make it easy to access when you're designing.

Moss

Moss can be kept moist and used live. Mist it often and keep it in the shade for use in a garden, on a table, or in a terrarium. Or you can dry moss by setting it on newspaper indoors. Dried moss can be used to make wreaths and embellish a number of indoor decorations.

Twigs

Twigs should be stored outside in a pile or an open container.

Vines

It's best to keep vines outdoors in order to maintain the moisture level needed to shape them into wreaths.

Live plants such as ferns can be transplanted to a terrarium.

The Right Glue

There are many types of glues on the market, suited to a variety of woodland art projects. It's always advisable to read a product's label to determine if it's right for the project you're undertaking. Here are a few types of glue frequently used in crafting and sold in most craft stores.

Silicone

This adhesive is water-resistant and a good choice for outdoor projects. Although it does take some time to dry, it has a thick consistency that holds elements in place fairly well while it's setting, and it ultimately results in a strong bond. Always wear gloves when using this type of glue, and keep in mind that silicone has a strong odor, which can make it undesirable when working on large projects.

Aleene's Tacky Glue

This all-purpose glue has a quick grab and works well for holding items such as shells, pinecones, pods, and twigs. It is one of the adhesives I use most often.

Quick Grip

Another all-purpose, quick-grab adhesive, Quick Grip is permanent, water- and weatherproof, flexible, and paintable, and it bonds to almost any type of material. It also dries crystal clear. The only drawback with this product is that it is extremely flammable, so be cautious when using it.

EcoGlue

This is an earth-friendly power glue that bonds with all types of wood, stone, metals, ceramics, and more. Besides being water-resistant and flexible, it is also heat-resistant and dries clear in about 20 to 30 minutes.

Hot Glue

A big selling point for this glue is that it dries almost instantly. For that reason, it's especially important to be well organized when using this type of glue. Be mindful, too, that it can lose its hold when subject to extreme temperature changes or a lot of movement. I sometimes add a touch of hot glue after applying stronger, longer-lasting glues, such as silicone or tacky glue, to hold the item in place while the stronger glue dries. The best hot glue gun to buy is Aleene's Ultimate Glue Gun, which lets you adjust the temperature to control the flow. It also comes with four different nozzles and an easy-to-squeeze handle for dispensing.

CHAPTER TWO

Twigs, Vines, and Roots

IT DOESN'T TAKE MUCH FOR WOODLAND MATERIALS to transform and enliven a space. It can be little more than the turn of a vine into an attractive wreath or assorted twigs fashioned into a chandelier. Nature enriches us by providing a wealth of materials to create with, and the results are often innovative, surprising, and thought provoking. In this chapter you will see a variety of artists' inspiring approaches to designing with wood and bark.

Patrick Dougherty's *Twisted Sisters* installation on the Wheaton College campus in Norton, Massachusetts, seamlessly weaves vines together into a building with multiple entrances and windows.

Garden Woodland Nymphs

ASSEMBLAGE ARTIST JANET COOPER has a real fascination with sewing, crocheting, knitting, and other handiworks — both the process and the materials. She regularly collects items such as printed fabrics from unfinished quilts, embroidered tea towels, sewing baskets, buttons, and vintage evening gowns for her art.

These woodland nymphs, designed to be used in a garden, are about four feet tall and are part of a series she calls "Quilt Ladies and Party Dresses." To make them, she collected branches and entangled bittersweet vines during her walks in the woods. She began each figure by forming a tripod of three or four branches, using garden twine and carpenter's glue to secure it. The nymphs' clothing, cut from fabric and tulle, was weatherproofed by dipping it in beeswax melted in an electric skillet and diluted with turpentine. The outfits were then embellished with dried flowers and bittersweet berries. These lightweight figures are staked to the ground with metal rods and can be left out year-round.

This unique homemade twig chandelier is electrified with simple exposed bulbs.

Mimi Krysiak created this simple tree branch room divider with a velvet curtain hung on large wooden rings.

Hay and Stick Folk

Lifelike hay and stick figures of people farming, playing with dogs, and dancing enliven sculptor Michael Melle's farmstead in Plainfield, Massachusetts. Inspired by a hero scarecrow in the book *Dog Years* by Günter Grass, Melle sculpted his first character in 1991. He sometimes dresses the figures in costumes to make them all the more realistic.

TOP LEFT
A wonderful collage of twigs designed to look like a group of dancing figures, by Chris Pollack.

TOP RIGHT AND BOTTOM
A wooden face, carved by artist Vladimir Bachinsky, is integrated into a vine-entwined entry-way designed by Olena Bachinsky.

Wreaths

THE WREATH DATES BACK TO ANCIENT GREECE. Being circular in shape, and thus having neither a beginning nor an end, it represented eternity and was worn by brides as a symbol of good luck and happiness. In later times, pine wreaths became popular as Christmas decorations; their scent was thought to drive evil spirits from the house. Vines are commonly used to make wreaths too. Grapevines are most typical, but you can also use honeysuckle, kudzu, sweet pea, or bittersweet vines. I have used young willow branches as well. Many of these vines can also be transformed into baskets, trellises, garden furniture, and fences.

Finding Vines

Premade grapevine wreaths can be purchased at most craft suppliers, but if you have access to woods or a vineyard, or you happen to know a backyard grape grower, you can collect the vines yourself. Grapevines should be collected after the grapes have been harvested and before the frost. Cut the vines into two- to three-foot lengths. Any longer and they'll be difficult to detangle from surrounding ones and transport home. A side benefit of cutting vines is that you're actually helping to protect the trees and other plants that the vines climb on and eventually strangle as they tighten their hold. Once you have your vines, remove the leaves but retain the tendrils, which will give the wreath an added decorative flair.

ECO TIP

Vines left outside should retain their moisture and flexibility, but if they seem too dry to bend easily, you can soak them in a tub of water overnight.

A Simple Grapevine Wreath

To make a wreath, use several lengths of vine to form a circle, binding the vine ends together with brown paper-covered wire (sold in craft stores). Next, weave more vines around the circle until the wreath is as thick as you like, securing them with wire where necessary. Now prune any unattractive pieces of vine with clippers. For the finishing touch, decorate the wreath with dried flowers, berries, nuts, or other woodland finds, attaching them with thin wire. If you're planning on hanging the wreath outdoors, be sure to choose weatherproof items.

This large grapevine wreath is adorned with yellow willow branches and has a a smaller wreath tied to its center.

Long-stemmed Queen Anne's lace flowers, picked fresh from the meadow and woven into the grapevines, make a charming summer wreath. The blooms will last about two weeks.

Juniper Berry Wreath

Juniper berries are the most wonderful slate blue and show up nicely against a background of cedar greenery. Wired onto a grapevine wreath, juniper makes a lush, attractive decoration for the holidays. Just be sure to collect the berries early in the fall before the birds eat them. I hung this wreath outdoors over my kitchen window and eventually all the berries were devoured — but I had a front-row seat to observe the feasting.

Potting Flowering Vines

Premade grapevine balls can be purchased at most craft stores and used to grow any type of climbing flowering vine, such as this passionflower vine. Begin with a planter that's large enough to accommodate the ball. Plant a young vine in the container, and then set the ball on top. As the vine grows, train it to weave in and around the grapevine ball.

Princess Pine Wreath

Designed by Marlene Hurley Marshall

I made this wreath by wrapping princess pine around a flat wooden form and tying it in place. I then added pinecones to complement the soft beige tone of the dried curly pine leaves.

Princess pine vine

Scissors

Flat wooden wreath form with six predrilled holes (sold in craft stores)

Hot glue and glue gun

Pinecones

Thin wire

1. Weave the vine through the first hole in the wooden wreath form. Then wrap the vine around the wooden form until you reach the next hole, and weave the vine through it. Continue in this way until the base is covered.

2. Wrap a second layer of vine around the wreath like a ribbon, hot-gluing the ends in place.

3. Hot-glue a few pinecones to the wreath.

4. Use wire to hang the wreath.

Princess Pine

Also known as ground pine or running pine moss, princess pine is an attractive vine that produces small pinecones and curly pine leaves that turn from green to soft beige when cut. Lightweight and shallow-rooted, it is easy to collect and can often be found growing under trees where grass is sparse and on compacted forest floors under leaves and pine needles.

Vine Furniture and Fences

OVER TIME, VINES CAN GROW VERY THICK and heavy, way beyond the desirable size for wreath making. In the hands of talented artists, they become baskets, fantastic furniture, garden fences and arbors, gates, railings, and more.

Crafted by artist Peter Thorne from 30-year-old bittersweet, this stunning rustic chair is a premier example of vine furniture.

Campsite Construction

Master craftsman and woodsman Peter Thorne often explores the woods in search of interesting stones and timber with which to design garden sculptures and furniture. He and his wife Sarah have also regularly camped on the Maine coast for the past 20 years. Finding material on the shore or in the woods and bringing it back to the campsite to create something that makes life more comfortable really excites Peter. "It's happenstance, spur-of-the-moment construction otherwise known as being 'in the zone.' When you can see it in your head, sort of, but until you stand it up, you really don't know what it's going to look like."

CLOCKWISE FROM TOP LEFT
This 30-year-old vine, found in the woods in the Berkshire Hills in western Massachusetts, provided artist Peter Thorne with the inspiration and wood to build a captivating chair (as seen on facing page).

Peter's hand-built ladder comes in handy for gathering apples to bake pie at his Maine campsite.

Peter's large worktable is supported by four birch logs and used for preparing outdoor meals when camping. The wooden top is covered with plastic to create a clean dining surface.

Woven Borders

Middle-school teacher **Gordon Pratt** lives in the charming village of Kinderhook, New York, where fox grapevine is extremely invasive. Gordon collected a large amount of the vine along Kinderhook Creek and used it to create a whimsical fence (at left) in the front of his home, a project that took him about two weeks. Gordon's original inspiration was the wonderful bottle-brush–buckeye root fence at Olana, the Hudson River Valley estate of the famed nineteenth-century artist Frederic Church. This curved perimeter fence (below) surrounds the original carriage drive circle, house, and grounds. The Persian-style home is now a designated National Historic Landmark and looks very much as it did when Church lived there a century ago.

Branching Out

For craftsman **Jack DeMuth,** finding and collecting the materials he ultimately turns into fanciful rustic chairs, benches, garden gates, and trellises is an art in itself. He may be strolling in the woodlands or canoeing along a stream when, as he puts it, the perfect limb or branch finds him. Though he may not be immediately sure exactly how he will use the piece, he stores it in his studio, where, invariably, he will walk by one day and feel inspired by its shape and size.

The pole for this lamp by Jack DeMuth is a yellow birch trunk with its exposed root married to a bluestone base. The box-shaped shade is made of copper, bronze, and silver wire hand-woven into a pattern of small blocks.

DeMuth used several different woods to make this hoop-back chair. The frame is alder, the curved seat pieces are red osier dogwood, and the vines that seem to joyfully grow from the top are bittersweet.

Fanciful Furnishings

Elaine Rush is a renowned antiques dealer and a consum-mate collector of folk art. She is known for her extravagant taste and considers her collection an important part of her home and her life in the Berkshire Hills of western Massachusetts. Elaine describes her occupation as being in the business of finding neat things.

RIGHT
A delightful wooden table lamp sports a shade trimmed with twigs that move like fringe.

BELOW
Hundreds of small pieces of wood adorn the base of this unusual folk-art table built circa the 1920s.

This dining room table has an exaggerated root base topped with marble.

CLOCKWISE FROM TOP LEFT

An extra-large hall mirror showcases a rare and masterful frame of natural cork.

A vintage table clock made from twigs commands space in Elaine's kitchen.

Made from curved saplings and featuring an ample seat, this grand and rustic vintage chair is a focal point in the den.

A rare vintage cabinet, artist unknown, boasts creative handiwork with bits of wood and vines.

A side view of the cabinet shows Asian influence.

Chairs (viewed from overhead) fashioned from pairs of deer antlers furnish the dining room area.

A Fanciful Fortress

Artist Patrick Dougherty was raised in the woodlands of North Carolina, where he grew to admire the natural lines of the tree branches and saplings in winter landscapes. He observed that birds inherently know how sticks can tangle, and it is this simple tangle that holds his work together. Consequently, Patrick's work has a mysterious windswept and monumental quality that immediately enchants the viewer. His first work, *MapleBodyWrap*, was included in the North Carolina Biennial Artists' Exhibition in 1982, and since then his art has evolved from single pieces to large-scale outdoor installations that can be found across the United States, Europe, and Asia.

I went to visit the Max Azria boutique in Los Angeles when one of Patrick's installations completely wrapped the building with swirls and eddies of willow saplings. It was a sensational installation that captured the breathtaking beauty of nature. Patrick describes the project as an opportunity to bring fashion, sculpture, and the natural world together in one place.

One of the fascinating elements about Patrick's work is the fragility and temporary nature of the elements he uses, many of which begin to fade over time. The life expectancy of his sculptures is two to three years, challenging traditional assumptions that art should appreciate and last forever. He compares sculpture to a good flower bed, both having their season. In this regard, he believes that artists' primary consideration should be to create the work they have always dreamed about.

Patrick's goal is to engage people by exciting the imagination. His works, which often involve addressing site-specific situations, are meant to be fully accessible to the community throughout the process, allowing the public to share the drama and offer lots of feedback as the work unfolds. In fact, Patrick collects the materials he needs with the help of many volunteers, usually residents who live near the installation site.

The *Twisted Sisters* installation shown here was constructed during a three-week residency at Wheaton College in Norton, Massachusetts, with the assistance of student volunteers attending seminars in drawing, design, public art, and sculpture. Located near the campus's Peacock Pond, the four-tower fortress looks like it may have blown in from an enchanted forest.

Patrick Dougherty's magical outbuilding appeals to a visitor's sense of wonder and adventure. The interior has a fairy-tale quality that makes you want to stay a while.

ABOVE
The *Twisted Sisters* installation appears comfortably ensconced in its space, commanding a strong yet gentle presence. The windows frame captivating views from both the inside and the outside.

LEFT
While walking in the woods, photographer Susan Oken discovered this wonderful stick house, undoubtedly the handiwork of children inspired by nature's offerings.

Impressive Architects

Somehow birds know enough to gather a vast array of materials for building nests in which to hatch and raise their young. Woven out of small pieces of grass, weeds, lichen, bark, and twigs, the nests are the right shape and size, sturdy, and secure enough to stand up to the elements. Birds are inventive and will substitute building materials if they fit the basic size and texture requirements. Bits of fabric, string, paper, and wire often show up in their structures. (The laws that protect birds in the United States are far more sweeping than most people may realize, so be aware that in some circumstances it is considered illegal to possess a bird's nest, even one that has been abandoned.)

ECO TIP

A study by the Cornell Lab of Ornithology in Ithaca, New York, suggests that wild birds relish crushed eggshells. The study found that birds are not getting enough calcium from natural resources because acid rain is leaching calcium deposits from the soil. Setting out cooked, cleaned, crushed eggshells will attract birds to your garden, especially females, because they are predisposed to greater calcium depletion due to the egg-laying process. The eggshells should be rinsed, baked at 250°F until dry but not brown, and then crushed and placed in a feeder, strewn on a stone wall, or sprinkled on a deck railing.

The Birdfeeder Hat Project

Erica Fielder is the director of the **Birdfeeder Hat project,** an inventive and delightful initiative that sponsors community events to raise awareness and promote peaceful coexistence with other species in the watersheds in which we live. During these occasions, attendees wear amazing papier-mâché hats with broad brims that hold birdseed and feeding trays. Styled by Fielder, these hats are also topped with crisscrossed twigs that serve as perches for birds to light and rest on. Fielder says that she's always amazed to hear from a bystander that what feels like a big bird landing on the hat is actually a chickadee or some other small bird.

Fielder's impressive credentials include an MFA in visual arts and years of continuing education in biology and geology. She lectures and teaches, and she organizes nature walks for both adults and children. Beginning in 1974, Fielder received a number of public commissions and grants for projects such as cofounding the San Francisco–based Ecology for City Kids program and creating school programs focused on art and the environment. Fielder says, "The central question within these realms is how can I, as an artist, encourage a cultural shift to ecologically ethical behavior and nourish integrated relationships with the wild blue-green Earth?" Her wish is to inspire adults and children to become guardians of the health and well-being of our environment with the aim of achieving a cleaner world for the future.

Erica Fielder's Bird Feeder Hat

Each of these hats is an individual work of art that takes about eight hours to complete. You can commission one from Fielder, who continues to make and sell them to further her cause around the country. Or, thanks to her generosity in sharing her method for fashioning these millinery eco-chic delights, you can create one yourself.

Tape measure

Round balloon

Plastic (for covering your work surface)

Newsprint or newspaper strips

Batch of papier-mâché paste (see below)

Small bamboo skewers

Twigs

Ribbon

Birdseed

1. Measure around your head and then blow up a balloon to that diameter. Cover your work surface with plastic to protect it, if necessary.

2. Create the hat cap by covering the top of the balloon with newspaper strips dipped in papier-mâché paste. To do this, dip each strip in the paste to thoroughly saturate it and then run it lightly through your fingertips to remove the excess. Apply four layers of newsprint, allowing each one to dry (this can take several hours) before adding the next.

3. Begin building a brim at the bottom of the hat cap with strips of newsprint. Continue building the brim, using bamboo to strengthen it, until it measures about three feet wide (big enough for a person to hide under) around the cap. Top it with an ensemble of twigs. Attach pieces of ribbon that will be long enough to tie under the chin.

4. When the papier-mâché is completely dry, pop the balloon. Now sprinkle the brim with birdseed, don your hat, and sit in a park, in the woods, or somewhere else you're likely to come in contact with birds.

Three Ways to Make Papier-Mâché Paste

Method 1: For a quick and simple paste, mix three parts white glue and one part water (if you're using thick glue, such as tacky glue, use equal parts glue and water).

Method 2: This method is inexpensive and results in a nice, smooth paste. In a saucepan, mix five parts water with one part flour and bring the mixture to a boil. Boil the paste for three minutes and then let it cool.

Method 3: Another alternative is to stir together equal parts water and flour without cooking. You can also use wallpaper paste powder or cornstarch in place of the flour.

Tips for Working With Papier-Mâché

- Adding a little salt to the paste will help prevent mildew.

- If you live in a very humid climate, add less water to the paste.

- For a light-colored hat, use strips of plain copy paper for the last layer of papier-mâché.

Woodland Mobiles

KEVIN INKAWHICH IS A LANDSCAPE GARDENER, sculptor, and painter who collects natural materials whenever he finds them and fashions them into mobiles of pinecones, eucalyptus leaves, seedpods, and dried leaves. Referred to as the "green thumb Calder" (after the famous American sculptor, painter, and mobile artist Alexander Calder), Kevin attaches the natural items to delicate wire armatures in such a way that they flutter individually within the composition. You could say his work infuses a breath of fresh air into the decor by playfully, and respectfully, bringing nature indoors.

TOP
Kevin Inkawhich's *Catalpa Speciosa* creates an interesting juxtaposition of a natural element with manmade objects.

RIGHT
This dynamic mobile by Kevin Inkawhich, located in Manhattan at Kips Bay, is composed of stainless steel thread, brass and copper wire, and plant material known as *Craspedia globosa*.

Woodsy Frames

The **unique picture frames** that craftsman Nick Nickerson creates for vintage outdoorsy paintings, vintage photographs, and mirrors seem alive with movement. He accomplishes this by fashioning twigs and big curls of bark in such a way that they seem to grow or jump from the face of the frame. Nick describes his work as a cross between sculpture and collage, inspired by a love of nature that began in childhood days spent in the woods and near the lakes and rivers of Massachusetts. He feels that his work is a partnership between him and nature, neither designed nor planned but rather evolving itself.

Roots in Design

THE INTERWOVEN FANNING PATTERN of tree and vine root systems is another element of nature that has traditionally inspired design. Root furniture dates back centuries in China, where artisans reflected their reverence for nature by using the varying shapes to create sculptures, garden benches, and grand chairs. The art form is proving equally inspiring to contemporary artists.

CLOCKWISE FROM TOP LEFT These antique hickory chairs feature sizable, comfortable seats and are an intriguing accent to any decor.

A tree root turned upside down makes a dramatic sculpture ready to mount and display.

Made with the roots from a rhododendron bush, this rare and highly collectible Victorian bench was most likely influenced by the Chinese. According to the collector, this type of furniture was typically painted black.

Artist and antiques dealer James Gottlieb, located in Hudson, New York, has a real flair with natural elements. A juniper bush root hung upside down and juxtaposed with a classical gold-leafed mirror makes an extraordinary composition.

While the head and feet of this Indonesian bamboo duck are distinctly carved, the body is a section of root that remains unhewn.

This curve-backed birch sapling chair is comfortable and lightweight.

This large head of Medusa was imported from a mountain village on the isle of Bali in Indonesia. It must have entailed a great amount of work to excavate the root mass and transport it to a village prior to chiseling the face. A great portion of the root system, left uncarved, serves as the Gorgon's snakelike hair.

Woodland Spirits

When Joan Meakin, a costume designer and lover of nature, needed to take time off from work to recuperate from a fall, she tried her hand at carving roots, inspired by the human forms she saw in them. These woodland root people, or "Woodland Spirits" as Joan calls them, are lovely, exuding a sense of joy and movement. She uses an X-Acto knife and a Dremel tool to create delightful faces on dancing root bodies, figures that reflect Joan's experience designing costumes for dance companies such as the Hartford Ballet in Connecticut and Jacob's Pillow in Massachusetts. (She has also toured with the Moscow, Bolshoi, and Stanislavsky ballets.) Carving a face is a process that goes very slowly, says Joan, taking several weeks to complete. The sculptures shown here (clockwise from top right) are *Running Man*, *Spirit of Jacob's Pillow*, *The Root of Joy*, and *Silver Birch Spirit*.

Woodland Faeries

Anna Brahms learned to make puppets and marionettes from a South African puppeteer while working for a puppet theatre in Tel Aviv. As her talent evolved, she began making dolls as well, some of which have been displayed in the windows of Tiffany's and Saks Fifth Avenue in New York. At first Anna made her dolls from wood, but she later switched to a modeling material that allowed her to carve more refined faces and fingers.

Anna has a deep connection to and love of the fairy world, which is reflective in her magical dolls. She clothes these little faerie-beings, as she calls them, in hand-sewn natural fabrics, and their tresses are made from real goat's hair.

Characters such as the old man faerie-being (upper left) are inspiration for story telling and meant to encourage children to imagine and dream. Tucked into a bed of moss and pine needles, another doll (below left) holds gathered fruit, while a third (below right) depicts a princess with eyes full of woodland dreams.

CHAPTER THREE

Pinecones, Acorns, and Seedpods

SEEDS ARE AMAZING WORKS OF NATURE, some soft, some miniscule, and each meant to be dispersed in nature, be it by the wind or animals, to start the cycle of growth. The outer shells of seeds are equally fascinating, designed to protect the seeds and then ultimately release them. The varied shapes and sizes of seed shells, casings, and pods make them interesting prospects for germinating woodland art.

Pinecones

PINECONES ARE THE FRUIT of the pine tree, and they come in a large variety of shapes and sizes. The hemlock cone is only about an inch long, while the sugar pine produces cones that are a foot long or more. Found in warm and cold climates alike, pinecones make a prime material to scout out for a woodland project. As seedpods go, the pine's are structurally complex, with many sectioned layers that open when the cone ripens to release the protected seeds inside. Even after pinecones drop their seeds, the cones are sturdy and will last for a long time.

RIGHT
A simple project with pinecones is to design number plaques for a house. First draw the number on a piece of wood, and then use carpenter's glue to attach pinecones, using sizes that suit the lines and curves.

Piney Garden Hat

To make this pinecone-encrusted garden hat, I applied tacky glue to tiny Eastern hemlock pinecones and stuck them to the underside of the hat's large straw brim, arranging them in circular rows. I encrusted the top of the hat with larger pinecones and orchid tree seedpods.

FACING PAGE, BOTTOM
Sarah Thorne is a window dresser and interior designer who curates and produces decorative arts shows. To create this woodland arrangement, she trimmed a basic grapevine wreath with pinecones, locust pods, and found turkey feathers.

Pinecone Mantle Medallion

This pinecone medallion (above) worked beautifully to liven up the wall space above my dining room mantle. I simply hot-glued the cones directly onto the wall, arranging them in a design of fiddlehead-style curls topped with a "tasseled" border. Occasionally a cone may fall off because of changes in room temperature, but I just glue it back on.

To create a medallion of your own (over a dresser or a bed, perhaps, or around a doorway), consider looking for a motif you like in a magazine or on a piece of fabric, and lightly pencil the one you choose onto the wall. Then cover the lines with pinecones or other woodland materials such as acorns, pods, and seeds.

CLOCKWISE FROM LEFT
A base of intertwined branches supports this handmade planter. The outside of the container is adorned with pinecone medallions and the interior is filled with fall meadow grass.

An impressive four-foot-high urn comprised of piñon pinecones wired onto a twig frame makes an attractive planter for a fabulous fern.

A simply adorned large pinecone serves as a curtain tie at the foot of a daybed.

Encrusted Pinecone, Bark, and Twig Mirror

Designed by Marlene Hurley Marshall

The earthy hues of pinecones, barks, and twigs glued onto a mirror frame can make a bold and attractive contrast to a reflected image, such as the outdoor greenery shown here.

Mirror with a solid frame (at least 3 inches wide)

Brown packing paper

Paintbrush

Tacky glue

2 screw eyes

Heavy-gauge picture-hanging wire

Blue painter's tape

Strips of flattened bark (consider pieces with lichen growth to add color and texture)

Hot glue and gun

Assorted woodland items, such as pinecones, acorns, and twigs

Brown paper-covered wire

1. Back the mirror with brown paper cut to fit the frame and glued in place with tacky glue.

2. Attach the two screw eyes to the back of the frame, one on each side. Thread heavy-gauge wire between them for hanging the mirror.

3. Tape the front edges of the mirror with wide strips of blue painter's tape to protect it.

4. Cover the entire frame with bark, fitting pieces together like a puzzle and gluing them in place with hot glue. Remember, you can cut most bark to suit your needs, such as to fit in a corner. Make sure the bark is flat so that it adheres well to the frame. Set the frame aside to allow the glue to dry thoroughly before applying additional elements.

5. Glue on your woodland items, balancing the types of materials you use in the four corners. If you choose to create fan shapes out of pinecones, as I did, start by gluing on three cones for the first layer. When the hot glue is dry, add a second layer of two rose-shaped pinecones. For the third layer, center a larger cone atop the previous layer. You can also use brown paper-covered wire to hold larger clusters of pinecones or twigs together before you glue them. The wire is great because it blends in pretty well, and you can curl the ends as part of the design.

6. When the glue is dry, remove the blue tape. If you notice any gaps where the mirror meets the frame, you can fill them in with thin twigs or pinecones.

Woodland Frame

VISUAL ARTIST ANN GETSINGER studied at Paier College of Art in New Haven, Connecticut, and the San Francisco Art Institute and has a multitude of creative interests, but she is most known for her surrealistic style of still life and landscape painting. Her works, which she calls stillscapes, are part of many private collections.

Ann's creative spirit is reflected in her delightful oil painting (at left) of an oak leaf falling from the sky, which she calls *Oak Leaf and Contrail 2008.* To complement her artwork, she decorated a swirl-topped luan mahogany frame with chestnuts, locust and iris pods, oak leaves, pinecones and needles, and maple bark. Topping the whole thing off is a glorious dried mushroom crown.

ABOVE
Small frames covered with curled pods and seeds from an orchid tree growing in crafter Sheila Luciano's Florida yard beautifully showcase a pair of family photos.

Pine Needle Basketry

The charm and ingenuity of this basketry style has a long history in America. African slaves were adept at stitching coil-wrapped grasses into strong, utilitarian baskets. In time, as grasses became less available, they began using pine needles. Likewise, some Native American tribes traditionally used pine needle baskets for cooking, storing foods, and gathering. Certain pines, including Ponderosa and Southern pines, produce needles five to eight inches long, which are picked while green, soaked for flexibility, and bundled in groups of six for basket weaving.

Hats Off to the Acorn

ACORNS ARE INCREDIBLE. Within one of these relatively small, capped seeds is the genetic material for an oak tree that can grow 80 feet high or taller! Chances are that a good many of the acorns you find will be separated from their tops, but you're likely to find the lids nearby. Simply glue them back on if you need whole nuts for your design. After collecting acorns, give them a rinse and set them out to dry.

Acorn Picture Frame

I made this acorn- and pinecone-topped frame (above) to add a woodland-style border to a favorite photo my son Michael took of an outbuilding on the family farm. The frame is a rich brown, which nicely matched the tone of the acorns. (Another option would have been to use a frame covered with burlap as a base.) When decorating the frame, I first attached the acorn caps, arranged in rows, using a paintbrush to apply tacky glue just to the rim surfaces that would rest against the frame. I used a second clean paintbrush to remove any glue that seeped out from under the caps. To fill the small spaces between the acorns, I then added the hemlock pinecones, which are about one-half inch in size.

Acorn Necklace

Robin Greeson is an artist and antiques dealer who specializes in ethnic jewelry and textiles. She created this dynamic necklace by fashioning used electrician's copper grounding cable into a bib of coils. She then drilled holes in assorted acorns and nuts collected in the woods surrounding her home and threaded them onto the wire.

BOTTOM LEFT
A charming pair of earrings made by Mariette Moon features acorns wrapped in fine copper wire.

BOTTOM RIGHT
Eleven-year-old Drew Tiano designed these cedar moth deterrents for closets and sells them at an upstate New York farmers' market. His father helped him cut the acorn and maple leaf shapes. Then Drew used his wood-burning set to embellish them.

CHAPTER FOUR

Moss, Greens, and Wildflowers

THE MORE TIME YOU SPEND IN THE NATURAL WORLD, the more aware you become of its wonders and contrasts: the colors of flowers, textures of leaves and grasses, and types of moss. The deep, shady woods, for instance, have a mystery and quiet, while meadows bordering a dense collection of trees have an uplifting openness. Whether tangible or spiritual, nature has much to offer a woodland artist.

59

The Magic of Moss

FOR CENTURIES MOSS HAS BEEN routinely planted in Japanese gardens, and as of late it has gained popularity as a low-maintenance substitute for many ground covers in other locales. In some circumstances, it even makes a viable alternative for grass. Its only requirements are shade and adequate moisture, since it gets the nutrients it needs from the air and reproduces when its windblown spores fall on moist soil. It's often found in the wild under trees and growing on rocks.

Moss Acres

Moss Acres is a unique company that ships substantial quantities of live moss to home gardeners, landscape architects, designers, and contractors across the United States. Owned and operated by Al Benner, son of the renowned horticulturist, professor, and "Moss Guru" David Benner, it is located on a 54-acre wooded hillside in the Pocono Mountains of

Pennsylvania, where several species of moss thrive. In the early sixties, the elder Benner began experimenting with using moss to replace the grass in his woodland garden in New Hope, Pennsylvania, and he has since covered more than two acres with moss and wildflowers. The Benners' moss garden has been featured in many books and magazines, and Dave still conducts tours.

Moss-Covered Garden Table

This lush moss-covered table (above) makes a lovely setting for a sunset cocktail hour on my shaded terrace. To craft one like it, you'll need enough moss to cover the surface of a metal, wood, or tempered glass café table by fitting the pieces of moss together puzzle style. Once the tabletop is covered, use a garden hose to saturate the moss with a gentle stream of water. Then dress up the perimeter of the moss with a skirt of ferns or leaves that drape over the table's edge. Or, for a longer-lasting border option, wire grapevines together to form ropelike trim (alternatively, you can purchase grapevine rope at a craft supply store). Fashion the vine rope into a large ring, securing the ends together with more wire, and use it to encircle the moss.

To maintain your moss table, keep it in a shaded spot and water it regularly as you would a potted plant. Routinely remove any leaves that may fall on the moss. If you live in an area that gets cold come wintertime, don't worry. Moss can survive freezing temperatures. Just place the table where snow will fall on the moss to provide the moisture it requires.

Gail Peachin made this patio decoration by covering a large Styrofoam ball with dried moss and a dotting of acorns.

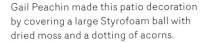

Planting Your Own Moss Garden

Fall is a perfect time to plant moss because the temperatures are cool and the weather typically supplies adequate moisture. Keep in mind that moss prefers acidic soil and shade. Once you have chosen a planting location, lay out the moss pieces as you would sod, pressing them into the soil and tamping them with your shoe to ensure there are no air pockets. Don't worry; tamping the moss will not damage it. When the pieces are all in place, mist them regularly (whenever it looks or feels dry) with a buttermilk and water mixture until the moss is established (approximately three weeks). After that, the moss will obtain all the nutrients it needs from the air.

If you have a large area that you'd like to cover with moss, or if you want to create a moss roof on a garden shed, it will be less expensive and less time consuming to broadcast bits of moss or mix and spread moss slurry. The advantage of using slurry is it allows you to quickly cover large areas while using less moss, but it can take a few weeks before the moss garden looks filled in. Slurry is also good for painting garden walls, large rocks, and garden pots.

A collection of many different kinds of moss collected for creating a moss-covered table was rinsed with a garden hose before being placed on the table top.

How to Make Moss Slurry

Combine two parts moss, two parts water, and one part buttermilk in a blender (preferably one that is not used for food).
Blend the mixture thoroughly. Spread the slurry mixture across
the whole surface of the area where you wish to grow moss.
Periodically mist the slurry-covered areas with water until
the moss is established. Then mist the moss annually with a
buttermilk-and-water mixture to keep the soil acidic enough for
the moss to thrive.

Shade and moisture are perfect conditions for moss to flourish. It's often found
in the wild under trees and growing on
rocks.

Landscapes in Miniature

Designed by Wenonah Webster

The enclosed worlds created by floral and garden designer Wenonah Webster include small hillsides, miniature rocks, and interesting plant combinations — works of art she considers to be "just gardening in miniature." Wenonah made this particular miniature garden-under-glass using a French apothecary jar. The plants (a small fern plant, a begonia, and African violets) are secured with moss.

Glass or plastic airtight container with lid

Clean gravel, pea stone, or coarse sand

Activated charcoal

Peat moss

50/50 potting soil (blend of soil and sand)

Kitchen spoon

Fern (a small specimen with limited growth expectancy is the best choice)

Other terrarium plants

Moss

TIP: *When choosing plants, Wenonah recommends selecting ones with similar light, watering, and humidity requirements. She also suggests varying textures, colors, and heights.*

1. Cover your work surface, if you wish, to protect it while you work. For the first terrarium layer, add pea stone, pebbles, or coarse sand to the jar. Fill it with two inches of gravel for a medium-size terrarium; use less if the container is small and more if it's larger.

2. Add ½ cup of charcoal to help maintain clean soil. Then add a ¼-inch layer of peat moss to prevent the soil from dropping down in the terrarium. For the final layer, add approximately three inches of 50/50 potting soil.

3. Plant your fern and then the other plants in the terrarium, using a kitchen spoon to dig small holes in the soil for them.

4. Cover the soil with moss, tucking it around each plant. Besides looking attractive, the moss will help maintain moisture. Add special stones or pieces of wood to complete your miniature garden design.

5. Water the plants until the soil is just moist, pouring the water down the sides of the glass container to clean off any soil on the sides. There should be no more than ¼ inch of water collected on the bottom of the terrarium. Put on the lid, but remove it periodically, when condensation appears, to let some of the water evaporate.

Terrarium Care

Water: Add water only if a terrarium seems dry, and then do so lightly. Use pure water, such as spring or distilled water, dampening the soil around the plants without wetting the leaves. Keep in mind that uncovered terrariums will need watering more often than those growing under a glass cloche, which produces condensation. Closed terrariums should be opened periodically to allow the moisture to dissipate and reclosed before drying out completely.

Light: Place the terrarium in bright, indirect or dappled light but not in direct sunlight, which can heat the air inside the container and essentially cook the plants.

Maintenance: If the plants become too large for the space, prune off the older leaves to encourage new growth, but do not fertilize them, since you want to discourage excessive growth. Plants that outgrow the terrarium entirely, become diseased, or expire should be removed and replaced. If you need to clean the inside of the glass, use only water and paper towels but no cleaners.

Terrariums provide a means of capturing and recreating a slice of nature to enjoy year-round. Plus they're ideal for people who are too busy to spend a lot of time caring for plants.

Basic Moss Wreath

Designed by Marlene Hurley Marshall

For this wreath (on facing page), I pinned live moss onto a ring of hay and then topped it with small crabapples and a pear to add color.

Moss (live or dry)

Straw wreath

Floral pins

Hanging wire

Decorative items, such as
    fruit or flowers

1. To begin, wrap a good-sized section of moss around a straw wreath and secure it with floral pins. Keep in mind that live moss will eventually dry but will maintain its color as long as it is not placed in full sun.

2. Add more moss, fitting the pieces together like a puzzle, until the wreath is covered. If you plan to hang the wreath on a door with glass panes, make sure the back is completely covered as well so that it is attractive from all sides.

3. Secure a hanging wire to the back of the wreath. Then use floral pins to attach fresh fruit, a fabulous ribbon, pinecones, or anything else that will complement your decor or appeal to your personal taste.

LEFT
Dried dusty blue hydrangea held in place with floral pins lends a simple but elegant look to a dry moss wreath.

BELOW
A wreath of bark, dried mushrooms, and moss, designed by Gail Peachin, looks at home on a rustic barn door.

Living Roofs

PLANTING SOD OR SEDUM ATOP BUILDINGS is an ancient practice that's been reintroducing its way into modern-day building practices. The Vikings of Canada lived in grass-covered houses, as have the Norwegians and Icelanders for centuries. And during the 1960s, Germany and its European neighbors began promoting the greening of rooftops as environmentally responsible. Today, New York City has a number of completed green rooftops and more in the works. The original Rockefeller Center roof garden, installed in the 1930s, is still flourishing. Industrial-sized green roof systems exist at Chicago City Hall and the Ford Rouge Center in Dearborn, Michigan.

Green rooftops have substantial and wide-ranging advantages over traditional roof surfaces. For starters, the insulating properties of living roofs result in lower energy costs. These roofs tend to get only about half as hot as exposed asphalt, significantly reducing cooling demands in warmer weather. And because they absorb a good deal of rainwater, demand on sewer systems is also lessened. The water they do release is relatively minimal and clean, having been filtered through the vegetation. Another advantage of green roofs is that they create wildlife habitats for birds and insects.

The cost of greening a roof can be approximately 50 percent more than that of installing a standard asphalt roof. Still, decreased energy costs and a longer life (these roofs last about 20 years) make them more cost-efficient in the end. In its efforts to encourage the greening of rooftops, Leadership in Energy and Environmental Design (LEED), a national organization with corporate headquarters in Colorado, will issue an environmental building certificate to builders who have met certain standards of green building. This certificate can be helpful in obtaining some financial assistance. Specific information can be obtained by contacting a LEED organization in your area.

This living roof, designed by Renzo Piano for the California Academy of Sciences building in San Francisco, is home to nine species of native plants.

Vertical Gardens

For more than 12 years, botanist Patrick Blanc has designed eco-conscious architecture using plants that grow on the interior and exterior walls of buildings. Drawing on his scientific background, he creates mosaics of plant life that adapt to, endure in, and enhance extreme situations. His vertical gardens can be found on buildings worldwide, including the French Embassy in New Delhi, India, the National Concert Hall in Taipei, Taiwan, and the CaixaForum Museum in Madrid, Spain. He has received many prestigious awards for his botanical surfaces, including Chevalier de l'Ordre des Arts et des Lettres and, more recently, the gold medal of the Academie d'Architecture.

Patrick's vertical gardens are composed of three parts. The base is a metal frame, constructed several inches away from the existing wall to provide air circulation. Next, thick sheets of PVC are riveted to the metal frame to make it rigid and waterproof. Finally, a layer of corrosion-resistant polyamide felt is stapled onto the PVC. The felt distributes moisture evenly and provides a surface on which the plants grow. The plant selections are made with consideration for the uniqueness of the space. A shaded parking garage, for example, is well suited for tropical plants.

These amazing systems (with the plants included) are lightweight, require no soil, and have no size or height limitations. Plus, they need very little maintenance — the irrigation system is automated, and the water is supplemented with nutrients.

A vertical garden installed in Paris is one of many throughout Europe designed by botanist Patrick Blanc.

Leaf Ceramics

DESIGNER ELLEN GRENADIER has been making tableware, custom tiles, and ceramic murals for more than 30 years. Her work is a stylish blend of refined forms and rich surfaces that are alive with natural color and texture. She currently produces stoneware that incorporates impressions of leaves, wild grasses, and Queen Anne's lace into elegant bowls, plates, sushi platters, dinnerware, and vases. Collecting natural elements is an important part of Ellen's process, and she has special trees and areas she favors.

She also freezes some of her materials so she'll have a ready supply throughout the winter months. Once the pottery is fired, the pieces are glazed with natural cobalt blues, copper greens, and ambers made from iron and then fired a second time.

BELOW
This beautiful tile backsplash, impressed with fern fronds, was designed by Ellen Grenadier and installed above the countertop in her country kitchen. It's easy to see why this work is one of her personal favorites.

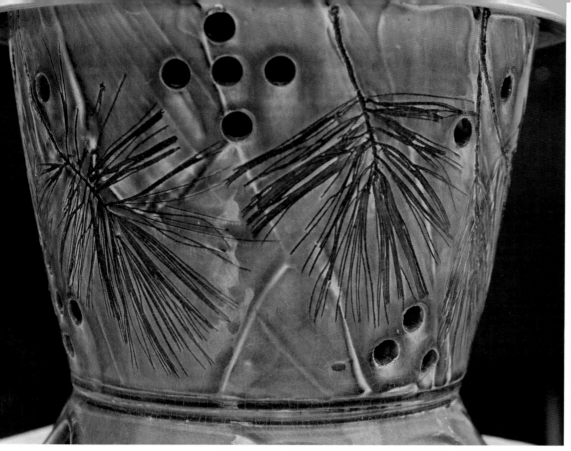

CLOCKWISE FROM TOP LEFT
Ellen used a pine tree branch to imprint this striking piece of pottery.

Ellen's fern leaf platter is finished with her signature green glaze.

Ellen uses Queen Anne's lace and wild grasses to embellish stoneware with a textured collage.

RIGHT
A small table with a nonglare glass top becomes a canvas for milkweed seeds framed with ginkgo leaves.

BELOW
Artist Linda Horn mounted dried Prairie Dock leaves to drywall to create this floating sculpture, evoking a lost landscape.

Flowery Hats

After working with clay for many years, artist Janet Cooper ventured into new media, turning found objects and vintage tin cans and bottle caps into wearable jewelry and fashioning whimsical pillbox-style hats from felt and flowers. The flowers come from the garden surrounding her home, where she grows irises, hollyhocks, Queen Anne's lace, coneflowers, roses, zinnias, peonies, lamb's ear, and lavender. After using silica salts and a food dehydrator to dry the blossom heads, she hot-glues them to handmade felt hat forms.

Whimsical Chairs

An upholsterer extraordinaire, Mimi Krysiak turned simple chairs into high-style interior decor using an imaginative choice of materials. She began by wrapping the chairs in a mustard yellow shade of soft suede, which she held in place with a piping trim made from twisted grasses. The unfinished edges create a frilled skirt under the seat and a cap sleeve effect at the top of the chair. Mimi hot-glued a fringe of dried hydrangea to the bottom of the skirt. The chair legs are wrapped with small, wine-colored eucalyptus leaves, while the chair back is adorned with larger eucalyptus leaves still on the branch.

Detail of reed grass piping embellishment.

Preserving Wildflowers

WHILE FRESH BLOSSOMS INSTANTLY BRIGHTEN any room, dried flowers provide a means of enjoying a touch of summer year-round. Not only do they look beautiful in an arrangement, they can also be used to make potpourri, decorate wreaths, and even design hats. Plus, flowers are fairly easy to preserve. Here are some helpful tips.

Harvesting

The best time in the season to pick flowers is just as they reach maturity. Don't wait too long or they'll go to seed. The prime time of day is mid-morning, after the dew has dried and before the blossoms wilt in the sun. Avoid damp flowers, which won't dry properly and may mold.

Air-Drying

The simplest way to preserve your flowers is air-drying. You will need a cool, dry room that is not too brightly lit. Secure each bunch (approximately a large handful) with a tie or rubber band around the stems and hang it upside-down on a rack for about a month. The exception is Queen Anne's lace, which should be dried upright. Flowers with weak stems can be supported with wire before drying. Smaller, more delicate flower heads, such as pansies and violets, can be pressed and dried between the pages of magazines or books.

Drying with Silica Gel

This granulated chemical can be purchased from a florist or in a craft store and can be used more than once. Pour some into a seal-able plastic or glass container that measures approximately 12 by 20 inches. Place the flowers, spread apart, on top of the silica gel crystals, and then sprinkle more crystals over the tops of the blossoms. Seal the container and set it aside for four days so the silica can absorb the flowers' moisture (you may notice the gel turns from blue to pink during this time). Avoid leaving them in the silica too long, or the dried flowers will be fragile. Or, if you're in a hurry, instead of setting the sealed container aside, you can microwave it for 3 minutes and then let it cool for at least 15 minutes. For stronger colors, use a smaller container and dry the flowers one at a time.

Carefully remove the dried flowers from the silica and gently sweep off the crystals with a soft brush. Once dry, you can spray the flowers with a fixative or hair spray to strengthen both the stems and the blooms. To dry the silica for reuse, bake it in the oven at 200°F.

OPPOSITE, TOP For this arrangement, I collected mullein flowers, milkweed pods, twigs, teasel, and iris pods, all dried by nature. The flower stems are held in place by small stones filling the bottom of the aluminum window box.

OPPOSITE, BOTTOM Wild violets grow in large clusters skirting meadows. These flowers will flourish in a garden but must be monitored to keep them from dominating it.

A bouquet of wildflowers, free for the picking, is ready to be styled into an arrangement or dried for crafting.

Making Potpourri

Basically, potpourri is an assortment of dried botanical materials, such as flower heads, leaves, pinecones, pods, moss, and berries, combined with a pleasantly scented oil. When it comes to the oils, a little goes a long way — 8 ounces can lightly scent about 500 pounds of botanical material. The only other thing you need is a fixative for retaining the scent. A fixative can be anything porous, such as wood shavings, bark, orrisroot, or a commercial product called Fiberfix.

Flower buds, petals, or leaves from your garden

Bits of moss or bark, acorns, pine needles, wild rose hips, or berries from a walk in the woods

Newspaper or paper towels

Scented oil

Fixative

Small nonporous bowl

Plate to cover the bowl

Large stainless steel mixing bowl

Paper bag

Tape or rubber band

1. To get started, place your garden and woodland finds loosely between newspaper sheets or paper towels to absorb moisture. Or you can dry them in an oven set at 100°F for about ten minutes, as long as you watch them very carefully. Just be sure your botanicals are dry to ward against mold.

2. To mix your potpourri, first blend your scented oil and fixative together in a small bowl. Cover the bowl with a plate and let the mixture stand for two to four hours.

3. Combine your botanicals in a big stainless steel bowl. Pour the fixative mixture over the botanicals and toss well.

4. Put the potpourri in a paper bag secured with tape or a rubber band and let it cure for seven days, shaking the bag daily. Transfer to a decorative display bowl.

Tips for Mixing Potpourri

There are all kinds of options when it comes to mixing botanical materials. You can combine large chunky pieces of neutral-colored barks, twigs, and pinecones in a birch bark or twig basket, and use a pine or sandalwood scent to create a woodsy blend. Or, for a more delicate combination, you might mix different-colored flower petals, such as lavender buds, baby's breath, and roses, in a crystal bowl or organza sachet bag and scent the potpourri with lavender or rose oil.

I mixed pinecones, star anise, sumac berries, pine needles, acorns, hickory nuts, twigs, small dried mushrooms, juniper berries, and small milkweed pods to make this potpourri. For essential oils, I chose sandalwood, clove, and cinnamon for a woodsy scent.

Queen Anne's Lace Dye

To prepare a dye bath using Queen Anne's lace, cut the flowers, leaves, and stems into short lengths and fill a five-gallon nonreactive pot with them. Cover the plant material with water. Boil the mixture on the stovetop for two hours, adding more water as necessary to maintain the level. Let the liquid cool and strain out the Queen Anne's lace.

Dying Wool with Queen Anne's Lace

Queen Anne's lace, also known as wild carrot, can be used as a natural dye when in full bloom. Surprisingly, this plant, with its lacy white flowers, produces a vibrant yellow hue.

5-gallon nonreactive canning pot

3 ounces alum

1 pound clean wool fiber, dampened

Queen Anne's lace dye (see left)

¼ cup tartaric acid or cream of tartar

½ cup Glauber's salt (see Resources, page 159) or pickling salt

Large wooden spoon

Tongs

Large strainer

Wooden hanging rack

1. Fill the pot with three gallons of warm water and dissolve the alum in it. The alum is a mordant, meaning it prepares the wool to accept and retain the dye. Add the wet wool fiber to the pot, place it on the stove over low heat, and simmer it for an hour. (Don't stir.) Then remove the wool, rinse it, and let it cool. Don't wring it out — roll the wool in towels to keep it damp until you're ready to dye it (you can keep it this way in the refrigerator for up to two days).

2. Gently push the prepared wet fiber down into the cool dye bath with a wooden spoon, cover the pot, and simmer (do not boil) the wool on the stovetop over low heat for 30 minutes.

3. In a separate container, dissolve the tartaric acid (to brighten the color) and Glauber's salt (to prevent bleeding of color) in one pint of hot water. Carefully add this mixture to the dye bath and continue simmering the wool for another 30 minutes. Let the wool cool in the dye bath, and then rinse it in warm water until the water runs clear.

4. Shake excess water from the wool and hang it on a rack in a shady spot to dry.

Once the wool is dyed, shake the excess water from it before hanging it on a rack to dry.

Natural Wool Dyes

Sara Burke grew up in Kentucky in a family of women who were always busy with some form of needlework, be it embroidery, knitting, sewing, quilting, braiding rugs, or just plain mending. "My love of fiber comes from their influence," says Sara, who also studied with fiber artist and master dyer Alma Lesch.

Sara recommends using a variety of natural materials to produce dyes of different colors. Here are some of her suggestions:

For red and pinks. Use bloodroot, madder root, or pokeweed berries.

For yellows, gold, and brass. Use Queen Anne's lace, onion skins, marigold blossoms, dandelion blossoms, dahlia blossoms, goldenrod blossoms, or zinnia blossoms.

For blues. Use elderberries or logwood chips.

For greens. Use turmeric, lily-of-the-valley, or sunflower seeds.

For lavender and purples. Use blackberries, Concord grapes, or mulberries.

For tan and brown. Use acorns, black walnut hulls, coffee, hickory sticks and bark, or tomato vine.

Wildflower Meadow Gardening

AT THE LADY BIRD JOHNSON WILDFLOWER CENTER in Austin, Texas, the staff's goal is to educate people about the environmental necessity, economic value, and natural beauty of native plants. One means by which they do this is to promote the concept of a meadow garden, a low-maintenance, beautiful alternative to mowing large sections of lawn. As an added advantage, a meadow garden provides food and cover for wildlife.

An important consideration when creating a healthy, thriving meadow is the ratio of wildflowers to native grasses. The Wildflower Center suggests grasses should be at least 50 percent of the garden. They provide support and protection for tall flowers, leave very little space for weeds, add texture, and prevent soil erosion. When choosing your perennials, annuals, and biennials, make sure none of your selections are on your state's noxious weed list. The Wildflower Center recommends against planting prepackaged wildflower seed mixes because you cannot be sure what you will end up with. Purchasing individual seed packets is generally the easiest and most affordable way to go. Go native whenever possible and strive for a variety of plants that will keep the garden colorful throughout the growing season.

The fall is the best time to till the ground and plant native plants, since perennials and some native seeds need a chilling period. Hand-broadcasting the seeds is the easiest method of distribution. Once scattered, rake or tamp the seeds into the soil. Before winter, remove any weeds that have made themselves at home and then leave the entire meadow standing throughout the cold season to provide food and cover for the wildlife as well as dress up the winter landscape. Come spring, mow your meadow and leave the clippings, which contain rich seeds, in place. As your meadow fills out, you may have to reseed or transplant in spots. The need to weed will taper off as the plants take hold.

When your meadow garden is in its third year, the Wildflower Center highly recommends a controlled burn. Fire is a natural process that helps control the growth of woody plants and invasive species, and it acts as a refueling force in many ecosystems. Surprisingly, the burning stimulates the growth of many grasses and perennials, and it breaks open dormant seeds. That said, the burning technique is one that should be directed or supervised by an expert. Many areas require permits, too. And in many urban areas, regulations prohibit controlled burns. If you cannot burn your meadow, continue to mow it each spring and spot-treat the weeds.

ECO TIP

Larry Weaner, a Pennsylvania landscape designer who has planted more than 100 perennial meadows, says the worse the soil, the better the meadow will be. Adding fertilizer, compost, or topsoil can actually lead to more weeds.

Prairie Painting

Artist and naturalist **Linda Horn** is a passionate advocate for the use of native plants. She also teaches conservation and meadow gardening. After moving to upstate New York from the Midwest, she bought a large piece of property and began cultivating a new meadow. She started with a controlled burn to cut the weed and seed population before introducing native plants. Knowing that a successful meadow must have a sizable portion of native grasses, she then seeded the ground with four major varieties: bottlebrush, Indian, Canada wild rye, and big bluestem. She also chose flower species found in the general region, among them bee balm, Culver's root (*Veronicastrum*), ironweed, spiderwort, black-eyed Susan, evening primrose, and New England meadow rue. Altogether, Linda's selections create an outdoor painting that is ever-changing.

Linda writes, "One part of the magic of native plant systems includes the intermingling of the plants to form an ecosystem. As insects and birds discover a newly created habitat, the support system for life is reestablished along with an aesthetic biodiversity unlike controlled gardens. This system is based on native seed ecotypes that have evolved in climates and soils specific to location. The refinements of seed selection can then be adapted to topography, soils, and human preferences. Gardening within this system adds the never-ending delight of discovery."

Linda Horn used her original meadow on her five-acre prairie in Michigan to create a sculptural installation, tying big bluestem and Indian grasses to create a line of arches. When she came back the next day, birds in need of material for nest building had untied all of the strings.

CHAPTER FIVE

Trees, Logs, and Bark

TREES STORE ENERGY, produce oxygen, sustain wildlife, and grace us with immeasurable beauty. The leaves alone display a spectrum of color, from lush green when they're newly unfurled to glowing golds and ambers as they fall from their branches in the autumn. The trunks serve as natural backrests for readers and dreamers on a summer day and provide us with wood for crafting fine furniture, making paper, and burning to generate heat in the winter. In the city or in the country, trees invite us to pause and enjoy the landscape.

Wild Trees

WITH TRUNKS THAT RISE as high as a 35-story building, the wild redwood trees that grow in the forests along the northern coast of California are one of the largest life forms that exist in the world today. The redwood forest is comprised of thick layers of soil, beds of ferns, and thickets of huckleberry bushes — not on the forest floor, but high in the canopies of the redwoods themselves. The reason this unique ecosystem exists hundreds of feet above the ground is because forest fires and lightning hollow out caves in the massive trunks, and over time the wood rots and turns spongy, creating an environment in these live trees where plants thrive.

The soil that lines these caverns is said to be composed of centuries' worth of decomposed lichens, twigs, and redwood needles.

The scientists who study these large trees invent ways to measure the height that range from using handheld lasers to having a climber run a fiberglass measuring tape from the base to the very top of the leaf growth. Scientists also regularly document the growth of the trees' trunks and limbs. Some even sleep in the trees or get married in them. When a scientist discovers a tree that is unknown and undocumented, he or she is invited to propose a scientific commission name drawn from mythological concepts, minerals, a place, a country, or a scientist.

BELOW
In his photographs of Sequoia National Park, Tom Zetterstrom pays respect to the grandure and endurance of *Sequoia gigantea*. It lives for up to three thousand years but only on the west-facing Sierras in a few dozen small groves.

Restoring America's Elms

Elm Watch is a Massachusetts-based program designed to motivate people to create greener communities. A particular focus is the restoration of the American elm tree, whose population has plummeted since the 1930s, when Dutch elm disease first arrived in this country. The fungus is transferred from tree to tree by elm bark beetles. Tom Zetterstrom, founder and spokesman of Elm Watch, grew up watching his father, a tree surgeon, treat a great number of diseased elms. As a high-school student, he helped his father cut down diseased trees or spray them with DDT, which killed the elm bark beetles (and many other things it came in contact with). Ironically, before Dutch elm disease began its run, the majestic elm tree had been a fixture in town and city environments because of its stress-resistant constitution.

After college Tom decided to leave the tree business and went on to teach photography. During that time, he began to notice that elm trees along the roadsides of Connecticut and Massachusetts were continuing to die off, and nobody seemed to be doing anything to correct the problem. Finally, he decided to take action, beginning with a single tree, a grand specimen located in Egremont, Massachusetts, that is still thriving today because of his efforts. Thus was the origin of Elm Watch.

Elm Watch encourages the formation of tree boards or commissions in towns to help bolster budgets for the treatment of tree diseases, and also to plant new disease-resistant elms and other types of trees. The organization also wants to develop green downtowns by cultivating roadside treescapes and strives to educate the public on the immense power trees have to enhance our property values, clean the air, and provide shade — all of which create positive community identities.

One of the ways Elm Watch suggests a community can begin is with an annual Arbor Day celebration. Community tree planting has a long history; some of the very first of these events took place in New England, including the area where Elm Watch is working today. In Sheffield, Massachusetts, in May 1846, one thousand elms were planted in just three days.

ECO TIP

It's said that trees can communicate, not in words, but with chemicals. For instance, the willow sends a chemical warning to neighboring willows when it is under attack by worms or caterpillars. This message stimulates its neighbors to increase tannin production, which makes the leaves impossible for the pests to digest.

BELOW
Tom Zetterstrom discovered this coast live oak (*Quercus agrifolia*), an evergreen, growing within view of the Pacific. Found from Monterey to Baja, this species is commonly wider than tall, with gestural branches sometimes reaching the ground and adding stability against the prevailing Pacific winds.

Tree Sculpture

AXEL ERLANDSON WAS AN AMERICAN FARMER who had an unusual relationship with trees. In 1925, near Turlock, California, Erlandson began grafting trees, bending four sycamores growing on a six-foot plot into a cupola he named *The Four-Legged Giant.* Encouraged by his success, he went on to create more complex designs. Working with birch, ash, elm, and weeping willow trees, he shaped the young, flexible branches into zigzags, rings, hearts, loops, and spirals. These shapes were held in place with frameworks that he removed once the forms were self-supporting. The process included grafting, pleaching (the art of training trees into a form), and other techniques he called trade secrets.

In 1946, Erlandson purchased a small lot in nearby Scotts Valley, California, and moved his trees there to develop a roadside attraction. He opened the Tree Circus a year later and delighted in showing his sculptures to passing tourists. He eventually sold the Tree Circus in 1963 and died a year later at the age of 79. Years later, in 1985, with the property in ruins and the trees destined for destruction, developer Michael Bonfante bought 29 of the trees. He had them root-clipped and earth-balled and moved them 50 miles to Gilroy, California. The trees now grow on a 75-acre botanical park as a memorial to the artistic imagination of Axel Erlandson.

A Sapling Seat

Arborsmith (or arborsculptor) Richard Reames, inspired by the work of Axel Erlandson, shapes living saplings into interesting sculptures, a craft he details in his book *How to Grow a Chair: The Art of Tree Trunk Topiary.*

Reames says it takes planning and patience to use this technique of sculpting with trees, but the results are worth the effort. He is developing a number of increasingly challenging designs, such as a spiral staircase growing in an oak tree, and a long-term project of growing a boat out of two very tall ash trees. Believing that people can appreciate the value in art projects that take time, even years, to come to fruition, he is even working on structures that will eventually become homes.

OPPOSITE, LEFT
Axel Erlandson standing next to his geometric living design tree in his Tree Circus.

OPPOSITE, RIGHT
A complex basket weave Erlandson created by planting a series of trees in a circle that were later grafted and pleached to achieve this interlaced form.

LEFT
Erlandson's Tree Circus, opened in 1947 along a well-traveled tourist route to Santa Cruz, California, featured over 55 uniquely shaped trees.

RIGHT
Erlandson's classic living chair was begun by planting four trees in a square and then patiently training them over time into a seat.

A Tree-House Home

Nic Osborne grew up in a home built with the clean, simplified lines of modern Bauhaus architecture, situated in the middle of some of the most beautiful woods in Connecticut. Needless to say, Nic wandered around those woods from childhood to adulthood, and his experiences greatly influenced his work as a dedicated artist/architect, woodsman, and environmentalist.

Nic and his partner Robin now live in a two-story tree house that he designed and built from the very woods that he was introduced to as a young child. The tree house reflects his dedication to the environment in every square inch of the exterior and interior. He kept an element of the Bauhaus influence by using many large windows, which gives a feeling of living in the woods. The basement of this magnificent tree house was built with massive tree trunks of white pine set on the rock ledge that already existed on the property. The basement door handles are large tree knots, a Nic trademark.

The exterior is a woodland wonderland of moss-covered trees that features a rock path dotted with wooden and rock sculptures, collected vines, and fallen twisted trees gathered and ready for the next creation. A balcony sits over a charming greenhouse adjacent to a nearby stone patio set up with tree trunk seats.

The interior was artfully and respectfully built with consideration for the existing environment, featuring tree trunks that seemingly grow up through the floor to the second story and a stair railing fashioned from twisted tree branches. The center island in the kitchen is a tree trunk on wheels, and the cupboards are equipped with tree knot handles. In the living area, shelves made from slices of a beech tree trunk are filled with found woodland treasures and sculptures made from nature.

A room off the kitchen, built completely from cedar, exudes a pleasant woodsy aroma. Nic told me he would have loved to build the entire house with this material, but it was not easy to acquire cedar in the quantity needed. This room has a feel of somewhere tropical, and it contains a very large canoe-shaped tree half perched on tree-knot feet and filled with woodland treasures.

OPPOSITE, RIGHT
The front entrance to Nic's tree house is surrounded by moss and stone and is set on a natural rock ledge.

OPPOSITE, LEFT
Double and single doors fitted with large tree knot pulls are the entrances for the tree house's garage and basement.

THIS PAGE, TOP
Stripped red cedar twigs create a rustic railing for a wide staircase leading to the second level of the tree house.

THIS PAGE, BOTTOM
Notches carved in a log accommodate multiple light switches.

OPPOSITE, CLOCKWISE FROM TOP LEFT
The dining area features shelves made from beech wood.

Nic built this sturdy center island-on-wheels for the tree house kitchen.

Red cedar posts and rafters lend this first-floor room a wonderful aroma. The walls are black cherry and the floor is white pine. A room-length sliced log mounted on tree knots serves as a shelf for holding a collection of woodland finds.

RIGHT
White pine tree trunks strategically placed throughout the house serve as major supports.

Woodsy Cottages

THIS MAGICAL COTTAGE (at right), built in the 1920s by a local woodsman with wood from the surrounding area, looks over a New England pond. To get there, you have to park about fifty yards uphill and then carry your belongings down a charming moss-covered root path to a small open clearing, where the cottage sits in all its splendor. The logs, which still have bark on them, are noticeably different from those of the usual log structures because they are all vertical. A small porch, featuring a birch log ceiling, overlooks the storybook pond.

The interior has a fairly large fireplace that is centered in the wonderful living room/dining room. The stairwell to the upstairs bedrooms is lined with logs, with a simple log for the railing, as well as, again, a birch log ceiling. The petite kitchen offers a built-in washstand in lieu of running water. Nonetheless, the owners have prepared many a gourmet meal in this lovely, secluded summer home.

RIGHT
Birch logs span the ceiling of the cottage's large main room.

OPPOSITE, BOTTOM LEFT
A tree branch strung with heavy twine provides a creative solution for hanging clothes.

OPPOSITE, BOTTOM RIGHT
A stairway leading to the upstairs bedrooms is still as solid as it was in the 1920s when the cottage was built.

Birch Porch

This unique enclosed birch log porch, designed by Don McAulay Sr. and his son Don McAulay Jr., is a favorite room where family and friends relax. Portions of the porch walls are built from full birch logs, and the domed ceiling features inlaid willow tree saplings framed in birch. The porch is also furnished with a birch-veneered grill equipped with acorn handles. Ironically, this woodsy design is just a stone's throw away from the heart of a bustling urban environment.

TOP
A handsome birch-bark-paneled cooking grill commands one end of the porch.

BOTTOM
This mortised branch chair with its refined triangle seat pattern and high ladder-back fashioned from twigs is part of a set of four.

A net of lights illuminates the birch framing of the porch's cathedral ceiling

Island Woodland

Artist Susan Oken lives on Martha's Vineyard in a home that's not only set in the woodlands but also inspired by it. The grounds feature handmade arbors and furnishings, such as a faux bois (cement carved to resemble wood) vintage bench, table, and stools. Living in this environment has prompted Oken to pursue her art, which includes wood carving and creating brilliant flower paintings.

LEFT
This railing was fashioned from found wood saplings. Despite its delicate appearance, it has proved to be very solid.

BELOW
A vine-covered arbor built from found wood provides welcome shade on a terrace.

LEFT
Walking alongside a river, I found this log with a large central cavity and brought it home to make this natural planter for wild violets.

BOTTOM, LEFT TO RIGHT
A large curved log with its center carved out and planted with sedums lines a garden pathway at Campo de' Fiori in Sheffield, Massachusetts.

A woodland figure built from logs and bark appears to be running out of the woods and scampering over a rock wall outside the home of artist Tyler Moore in Sheffield, Massachusetts.

Thin spheres cut from birch logs are glued to the front of a stately closed-up fireplace.

Standing People

Native Americans lived close to nature. Recognizing the special attributes of the birch tree, they used it to build canoes and wigwams (birch bark is naturally waterproof) and craft musical instruments, children's sleds, and hunting and fishing gear. For food, they foraged for many different types of greens, mushrooms, nuts, and berries. When other food sources were scarce, they used the inner portion of bark, which is full of starches, sugars, and vitamins and minerals, to make bread. They also relied on the skins of animals to make clothing and blankets, and they used other natural elements to make paints for artistically documenting their history as well as embellishing their homes and clothing. The Native Americans' reverence for nature was particularly evident in the mystical powers they attributed to trees, which they referred to as the "Standing People." They believed that the birch held the essence of truth, that the pine embodied peace, and the ash brought peace of mind.

Classic Canoe

Craftsman **Henri Vaillancourt** builds birch bark canoes much like those that were crafted by the Abenaki, Malecite, and Algonquin Indians and the ones developed by the French during the fur trading period. Vaillancourt's work has been on exhibit at the Smithsonian Museum and the World's Fair in Montreal. He and Todd Crocker founded the Trust for Native American Cultures and Crafts, a nonprofit organization dedicated to the recording and perpetuation of materials integral to northern Native American cultures.

RIGHT
This birch bark canoe was custom-designed for outdoorsman John Manikowski by artist Henri Vaillancourt. It is 11 feet long, lightweight, and small enough to manage alone. John uses it mainly for fishing, hunting, and recreation.

BELOW
Hands-on activities such as tree-planting workshops are great educational experiences for young children (like Carter, pictured here). Physical and tactile immersion in nature can build in them an appreciation for the artistic wonder of the natural world.

Barking Up the Right Tree

TREE BARK IS ANOTHER MATERIAL that is available year-round. And since it comes in a spectrum of colors, textures, and patterns (even within the same species), it lends itself to a variety of crafting projects. When collecting it, look for dead or fallen trees, which are the easiest and best to peel bark from. Removing bark from a living tree will threaten the tree's health. When you get it home, lay it flat and weight it down to keep it from drying further and curling up. This will make it easier to work with when you're ready.

If you need a substantial amount of a specific type of bark, you'll need to look for a grouping of fallen trees. At one of the nature preserves where I walk my dogs and hunt for materials, I once noticed that the maintenance crew had taken down a large dead tree and cut it up into three-foot lengths. They had then cut a line directly down the bark, creating a zipper-like opening. As time went by, the tree began to dry and the bark popped open, producing a supply that was plentiful and easy to gather.

If you have a hard time finding bark, you can always order some online. Birch in particular is readily available and comes in three dynamic colors: white, silver, and a glorious yellow that looks like it was dusted with gold. And because birch is thinner than many other barks, it can easily be cut to fit the size you need. You can even find it in cylinder form to fit directly around a similar-sized vase.

Birch Birdhouses

Inspired by organic forms and his admiration for the works of Andy Goldsworthy and Antonio Gaudi, craftsman José Pimentel builds one-of-a-kind birdhouses. He starts with basic premade frames that measure about two feet square and uses hot glue to cover them with birch bark sent to him from friends living all over the country.

A Birch Birthday Cake

Gail Peachin whipped up this earthy delight by cutting a wedge out of a thick round of Styrofoam to create a cake shape with a piece sliced out of it. She "frosted" it by hot-gluing on bark and moss and topped the whole thing off with pinecones and acorns.

Birch Curtain

A **talented painter and sculptor,** Susie Hardcastle routinely draws from nature for inspiration. Susie paints animals and other organic forms on fabric to create wall hangings, bedcovers, and pure silk, wearable-art scarves. One of her series features large (six- by five-foot), hand-colored drawings of wild animals such as deer, water birds, and monkeys. The attractive curtain at right, made by hot-gluing and stapling strips of birch bark into links, is designed to be used as a porch screen or an indoor room divider.

ABOVE
This vintage moose antler chandelier spans approximately four feet and features birch bark lampshades.

LEFT
Yellow lichen encircles the opening to a birch-bark-covered birdhouse designed by artist Len Campanale.

OPPOSITE, CLOCKWISE FROM TOP LEFT
A large piece of bark with curled edges and eyeholes instantly enhances a plain wall.

Artist Anne Fredericks hot-glued layers of small birch bark squares to a garden pot, creating a dynamic, multihued planter for summer flowers.

I used a hay wreath wrapped in burlap for the base of this bark-and-lichen-encrusted wreath and then filled in the gaps between the bark with pinecones, berries, and moss.

This spaceship bird feeder designed by Quinn Doherty (age 12) and Henry Doherty (age 9) is built from a small stump topped with bark, pinecones, and moss to provide a soft resting spot.

Bark Vase

Designed by Marlene Hurley Marshall

Pieces of bark completely transform a pedestrian container into an attractive textured vase for a bouquet of wildflowers.

Vase (metal, glass, or plastic)

Strips of bark

Scissors (to cut the bark)

Hot glue and gun

Tacky glue

Brown paper-covered wire

Several pinecones and acorns

1. Hot-glue pieces of bark onto the vase, then apply tacky glue to reinforce them. Keep in mind that while the bottoms of the bark strips should line up evenly so the vase will stand up straight, you can vary the height of the tops above the container's rim to create a rustic effect.

2. If some of the bark strips aren't long enough, extend them by adding shorter pieces. Use additional bark to bridge any gaps between the strips applied in the first round.

3. Tie a "ribbon" of paper-covered wire around the vase to further secure the bark. Then glue or wire a few pinecones or acorns to the wire to give the vase a decorative accent. Or you can simply curl the wired ends to resemble fiddleheads.

Woodsy Vessels

Carole Clark is a chef, gardener, and artist who enjoys foraging
for wild edibles as well as for bits of lichen, moss, bark, and dried
mushrooms with which to create unique vessels. To craft one,
she uses a hot glue gun with a flat dispenser head to cover a glass
or plastic vase with pieces of bark. She then adorns the top with
tiny mushrooms, a bit of green moss, dried cockscomb flowers,
or small berries. Once the glue sets, she uses tweezers to remove
any trailing strings.

CHAPTER SIX

Wild Edibles

EATING WILD FOODS is certainly not a new concept. After all, our forefathers did it. As food costs rise, it's a sensible pastime today. Plus, foraging for wild edibles is a wonderfully rewarding experience. Just think of wild greens, mushrooms, roots, berries, and flowers as produce straight from Mother Nature's farm. For the beginner, there are many good books, filled with helpful photos, about foraging for and cooking with these natural treats. Being a visual person, I always feel better being shown by someone knowledgeable what plants can be picked and eaten. And of course you'll want to find out whether the area you plan to harvest has been sprayed with pesticides or not.

Mushrooms

MUSHROOMS BELONG TO THE VAST WORLD OF FUNGI and vary widely. There are mycological associations all over the world that put out newsletters and sponsor seminars, research institute courses, and festivals to educate people about mushrooms. Some even organize forays into the woods to scout out and collect mushrooms for scientific research as well as to eat. Most of these association members call themselves "social 'shroomers."

It would take an entire book to discuss all the aspects of these fungi. There are so many types, and in some cases the differences are very subtle. To be safe, any person interested in foraging for mushrooms needs to be highly versed in which are edible and which are poisonous. I do not cover the topic in this book and strongly encourage going with an expert should you decide to harvest mushrooms.

Edible mushrooms, besides being flavorful, have many health benefits. Researchers at Penn State University found that portabellas and creminis rated as high in some antioxidants as the top-rated red peppers. Button mushrooms were not quite as high but still rated higher than tomatoes, carrots, and green beans.

Mushrooms and lichens are some of the strangest and most beautiful forms found in nature, but many are dangerous to handle or eat, so be sure to forage for them only in the company of an expert.

Ground-Breaking Fungi

Mycologist and visionary biologist Paul Stamets is the owner of Fungi Perfecti, located in Olympia, Washington, and the author of several books, one of which is *Mycelium Running: How Mushrooms Can Help Save the World.* Stamets lectures extensively on revolutionary ways to use fungi, particularly mushrooms, for solutions to save the environment. Mushrooms have the ability to decompose plants and animals, creating soils, and are therefore an essential element to the food web of life. He suggests that gardeners use fungi to promote and maintain fertile soil and enhance sustainability.

Hen of the woods (a.k.a. maitake, *Grifola frondosa*) is an amazing large and edible mushroom prized by foragers and considered a delicacy by foodies. It is typically found growing at the base of red or black oak trees.

Hen of the Woods (a.k.a. Maitake) Ragú with Polenta

Clayton Hambrick, chef/proprietor of the Church Street Café in Lenox, Massachusetts, has been cooking with wild mushrooms for 20 years. This appetizer for four is one of his recipes.

2 tablespoons unsalted butter

1½ pounds cleaned hen of the woods (maitake) mushrooms, sliced into ½- by 3-inch slices

2 cloves garlic, thinly sliced

½ cup dry white wine

2 tablespoons tomato paste

1 cup rich chicken stock

Salt and pepper

2 cups cooked soft polenta, warm

Grated Parmesan

1. Melt 1 tablespoon of the butter over medium heat in a large skillet. Add the mushrooms and garlic and sauté 8 to 10 minutes, until lightly browned and the liquid evaporates.

2. Add the wine and cook until the liquid is reduced to 1 tablespoon, about 5 minutes. Then add the tomato paste and stock and simmer the mixture until the liquid reduces by half, about 10 minutes.

3. Remove the pan from the heat, add the remaining butter, and season with salt and pepper.

4. Ladle the mushrooms over the polenta and top with grated cheese.

Sautéed Mushrooms

Carole Clark is a world-class chef and the former owner of Charleston restaurant in Hudson, New York. She is also a collage artist who forages for mushrooms and collects bark, moss, twigs, and lichen for her work (see page 105 for examples). Here is a tried-and-true recipe she recommends for most wild mushrooms.

Wild mushrooms

Cooking oil

Unsalted butter

Fresh tarragon

Fresh thyme

Salt and pepper

Dry white wine

Heavy cream (optional)

1. Remove the stems from the mushroom caps. (You can save the stems to make a flavorful stock, sauce, or soup.) Cut the caps into ¼-inch slices.

2. Sauté the mushroom slices in equal portions cooking oil and unsalted butter until they no longer release any liquid and are lightly browned.

3. Add chopped fresh tarragon and thyme and then salt and pepper to taste.

4. Moisten the mushrooms with dry white wine and cook them over low heat until tender. Stir in a splash of heavy cream, if desired.

5. Serve the mushrooms over toast, risotto, pasta, or a baked square of puff pastry.

Puffballs

These mushrooms are edible when they are young and firm. Avoid those with tough outer skins. Before eating them, slice them open to be sure the interior flesh is white. Puffballs with dark flesh should be discarded. Another important reason for slicing one of these mushrooms open is to be sure it is not actually an immature amanita, which is a very poisonous mushroom variety. Puffballs are best sliced and steamed, simmered in soup, or sautéed with garlic and onions in butter or olive oil. A good vegetarian source of vitamin D, they're reportedly excellent for breaking down cholesterol.

I found this particular puffball specimen under a large pine tree, surrounded by pine needles. Puffballs found in well-fertilized fields or pastures in late summer through midfall can grow as big as a soccer ball.

Chicken of the Woods

Chicken of the woods (a.k.a. sulphur shelf) mushrooms often appear strikingly bright against the tree bark it grows on. These mushrooms, which range in color from yellow to orange, can cause an allergic reaction or may not agree with some people's digestive systems. Keep in mind that this variety (*Laetiporus sulphureus*) can be nearly indistinguishable from many other *Laetiporus*, so be sure to collect them only when accompanied by an expert.

Morel Mushrooms

Morels have such an interesting texture. Pitted and ridged, these cone-shaped mushrooms resemble a sponge and come in various sizes and hues ranging from tan to dark brown. You can buy morel mushrooms at many farmers'

markets and gourmet grocery stores, but harvesting them from the woods is delightfully satisfying as well as less expensive. I went hunting for morels for the very first time while working on this book, guided by chef Sarah Dibben, who's an expert at mushroom identification.

The morel is one of the most favored of mushrooms among great chefs worldwide. A distant relative of the highly prized truffle, it grows in clusters, usually at the base of a tree. This mushroom must be cleaned well when harvested because of all the pockets where dirt can collect inside the head. It has a smoky, nutty flavor, and the darker the morel, the stronger the flavor. Morels can be breaded and fried, baked, stuffed with dressing, or simply sautéed in butter for about five minutes on each side.

Woodland Chef

SARAH DIBBEN WAS RAISED NEAR KANSAS CITY and started working in restaurants at the age of 16. Now the head chef at the Stagecoach Tavern in Sheffield, Massachusetts, she's known for her hearty cooking. In her early days of apprenticeship, she learned the value of choosing ingredients that are local and seasonal. She also became adept at preparing many wild edibles, a practice she has widely continued in developing dinner menus at the Stagecoach Tavern. (See her recipes beginning on page 112.)

On an early spring morning, Sarah Dibben, chef at the Stagecoach Tavern in Sheffield, Massachusetts, took me on a hunt for morels, knotweed, garlic mustard, and ramps. Back in the tavern kitchen later that day, the wild edibles were prepared for dinner.

Risotto Topped with Sautéed Morels

Risotto topped with sautéed morels picked earlier in the day is one of Sarah Dibben's dinner specialties. Here is her recipe, which makes enough to serve four. (Pictured with fiddlehead ferns added.)

6 cups water

2 bay leaves

5 tablespoons butter

1 medium white onion, finely diced

1 clove garlic

1 cup arborio or carnaroli rice

½ cup white wine, at room temperature

Pinch of salt

1½ to 2 cups sliced morel mushrooms

Chopped parsley or chives

1. Combine the water and the bay leaves in a saucepan. Bring the water to a simmer and then shut off the heat. Meanwhile, melt half of the butter in a heavy, high-sided saucepan over medium heat and cook the onion and garlic in it until they are slightly browned.

2. Add the rice to the onions and garlic and lightly toast it for 2 to 3 minutes. Add the wine. Stir the mixture until all the wine is absorbed.

3. Ladle in just enough of the warm bay-infused water to cover the rice (roughly ½ cup). Stir constantly until the water is absorbed. Repeat this step until the rice is al dente. (This takes about 20 to 30 minutes. You may not need all the bay-infused water.) Season the rice with salt to taste.

4. While the risotto is cooking, sauté the morels in the remaining butter over medium heat until tender.

5. Spoon the rice onto a serving dish and top it with the morels and a sprinkling of parsley or chives.

Chef Sarah Dibben introduces her young son, Emery, to the morel mushroom while out on a foraging trip.

Japanese Knotweed Chips

Sarah Dibben's fried Japanese knotweed chips are a delicious payoff after a day of foraging.

Young Japanese knotweed cuttings
Vegetable or canola oil
Sea salt

1. Remove the Japanese knotweed leaves from the stalks. Wash and dry them well. Discard the stalks.

2. In a high-sided saucepan over medium-high heat, or using an electric deep fryer, heat about ½ inch of oil to 350°F. Place a few leaves in the hot oil and let them sizzle for about 45 seconds to a minute, depending on their size.

3. Remove the leaves from the oil and place them on a towel to drain. Repeat with the remaining leaves. Sprinkle the leaves with sea salt while they're still hot and serve.

Japanese Knotweed

Japanese knotweed is yet another wild food that can be harvested in the spring. The asparagus-like skinny young shoots, the young leaves, and the peeled larger and fatter young stalks are edible and have become a new haute cuisine item for creative chefs to add to their menus. Knotweed is actually an invasive weed native to eastern Asia and Korea, and it is an invasive plant here as well, so you don't need to worry about harvesting too much of it. Originally introduced to North America for ornamental use and to prevent soil erosion (it can tolerate all types of soils), it can be found growing along roadsides and riverbanks. Knotweed (especially the dried stalks from the previous year's growth) looks very much like bamboo except the shoots and young stalks have little red spots on them.

Ramp Festivals

Ramps are considered a spring staple in the mountain regions of the eastern United States and are especially popular in Tennessee, Pennsylvania, Ohio, West Virginia, North Carolina, Kentucky, and Virginia. Spring ramp festivals have been held in these regions for decades, featuring music, dancing, bountiful food, ramp tramps (foraging for ramps), ramp-eating contests, recipe books, and the annual crowning of the "Maid of Ramps." More recently, Slow Food USA, a volunteer collective of farmers, business owners, and community residents, has lent its support to these festivals as a means to perpetuate its mission of promoting local, ecologically sound food production as well as awareness of the importance of wild foods.

Ramp Bread Pudding

Sarah typically serves this recipe with braised chicken surrounded with a pool of broth. It serves six to eight depending on the portion size.

10 eggs

5 cups whole milk

1 tablespoon chopped fresh garlic

2 teaspoons salt

Black pepper

4 cups ¾-inch bread cubes (cut from day-old bread)

3 cups ramps, greens only (note: you can use the ramp bulbs for pickling)

1. Whisk together the eggs, milk, garlic, salt, and black pepper to taste in a large bowl.

2. Gently stir the bread into the egg mixture and let it soak for an hour.

3. Preheat the oven to 300°F. Cut the ramp leaves into 1-inch pieces, and fold them into the bread and egg mixture.

4. Butter a 9- by 13-inch baking pan and pour the bread pudding into it. Bake the pudding until no liquid rises to the top when you press down on the middle, 45 minutes to 1 hour.

Ramps

The ramp (*Allium tricoccum*), also known as a wild leek, is a member of the onion and lily family. Ramps are some of the first greens to sprout in the very early spring, and their season is eagerly awaited by many chefs who consider ramps to be a delicacy. Sautéed ramps are often used in place of onions to create a more piquant dish. Another popular way to prepare wild ramps is to pickle them. Be aware, though, that overharvesting ramps may wipe out patches of the plant as well as create opportunities for invasive plant species to establish footholds in pristine woodlands. Generally, it's a good idea to harvest the ramp leaves only, and leave the bulbs in the ground to minimize soil disturbance and ensure the continued local availability of ramps over the long term.

Sarah Dibben is adept at creating delectable dinner menus from wild edibles collected earlier in the day. Here, Sarah's ramp bread pudding is served with braised chicken.

Sarah Dibben's Pickled Ramps and Fiddleheads

Pickling is a good means of preserving wild edibles such as fiddleheads and ramp bulbs.

Fiddleheads and wild ramp bulbs, enough to fill
    2 pint jars

2 pint-sized, widemouthed glass canning jars

1 cup white vinegar or cider vinegar

¾ cup water

½ cup sugar

¼ cup kosher salt

2 bay leaves

10 to 12 whole black peppercorns

1. Prepare your wild edibles for pickling by making sure they are thoroughly clean. A good method for cleaning fiddleheads is to soak them in water; any soil will fall to the bottom, while the fiddleheads will float. Then lift them gently out of the water, rinse them extra well (you'll want to remove the brown, papery husk, which is inedible) and set them aside to dry on paper towels. For ramp bulbs, snip off the tops about ½ inch below where the green starts. (Save the green leaves for making soup, a sauté, or the savory bread pudding on page 114.) Rinse the bulbs well and set them on paper towels to dry.

2. Pack the clean and dried fiddleheads or ramp bulbs into the glass canning jars.

3. In a stainless steel pot combine the vinegar, water, sugar, salt, bay leaves, and peppercorns and bring the mixture to a boil.

4. Ladle the pickling liquid over the ramp bulbs or fiddleheads covering them completely. Allow the jars to cool and then tightly screw on the lids. Refrigerate the jars for up to three weeks to allow the pickled fiddleheads and ramp bulbs to age.

Fiddleheads

Fiddleheads are the young coiled leaves of the ostrich fern (*Matteuccia struthiopteris*), harvested in early April and early May, as soon as the tender little rolls have sprouted an inch or two above the ground. Ostrich fern is sometimes found growing among bracken fern, which looks very similar and can be poisonous, so it's a good idea to consult an expert before harvesting them, as is the case with any wild foods.

To prepare fiddleheads for eating, carefully brush away the brown paperlike scales, trim any stems below the heads, and then wash and steam the heads in a small amount of water for about 20 minutes. You can serve fiddleheads as is with melted butter, turn them into a pesto, add them to a soup, or pickle them.

Maple Sugaring

Susan Schwartz, owner of Strawberry Farm in Savoy, Massachusetts, started making maple syrup nearly 25 years ago when she and her husband built a sugarhouse on their small farm. The annual sugaring process begins in late February and goes through March, when the nights are typically still cool and the days are warmer — prime conditions for sap to start running from the sugar maples. Susan taps the trees and hooks on buckets for collecting the sap. Once full, the buckets are brought by sleds to the sugarhouse, where the fresh sap is cooked down to maple syrup. It takes about four hours to boil down 40 gallons of sap. The syrup, which is stored in glass jars, has a shelf life of about three years.

Susan also produces maple cream, a sweet spread that has the consistency of soft fudge. To make it, she boils syrup to 225° F. As it cools and sets up in the jars, the syrup thickens and becomes creamy.

Sarah Dibben's Wild Grape Jelly

In some parts of the country, wild grapes are called frost grapes because they're not ready to harvest until wintertime. If you're lucky enough to get some before the birds eat them, they can be turned into a delightful jelly using Ball No Sugar Needed Fruit Pectin.

Simply combine 2½ pounds of grapes with 1 cup of water in a large saucepan. Bring the water to a boil, then reduce the heat to low and let the fruit simmer for 30 to 40 minutes. Strain the liquid through a fine-mesh strainer or double layers of cheesecloth. Now follow the instructions for grape jelly on the pectin package.

This kind of pectin allows you to use much less sugar than the 5 to 7 cups normally called for in traditional recipes, and your jelly will still set up with a good thick consistency. Keep in mind, though, that wild grapes will need a little more sweetener than cultivated grapes.

For a naturally sweet treat, Sarah makes two preserves: one with wild grapes, the other with wild strawberries in rose petal jelly.

A World of Wild Edibles

IT'S AMAZING TO DISCOVER how many common wild plants — some of which we often think of as weeds — offer interesting culinary possibilities.

Dandelions

Once considered a bothersome weed and a menace to lawns, dandelions are now displayed with pride in the produce section of gourmet grocery stores. When I was a young child, I would see older folks by the roadside picking these seemingly ordinary weeds. Little did I realize at the time what a valuable food source these weeds are. Dandelion leaves are best picked before the plant blooms, when they are still tender. They can be served raw in a salad or steamed as a vegetable. When the bright yellow flower blooms it too can be harvested to make jelly or even dandelion wine.

Daylilies

The daylily (*Hemerocallis* spp.) is a great wild food. Recognizable by its bright orange flower, it is often found along country roadsides and in old gardens. The early shoots, flower buds, and flowers are edible. Add them to a salad raw or dip them in batter and fry them as a tempura dish. Their texture is very much like that of okra. Make sure the ones you eat have not been treated with any type of chemical. Also, be aware that some people may find that daylilies do not agree with their digestive systems.

My Candied Violets

Although this can be a time-consuming project, the results are most gratifying. The sugary treats can be used to decorate cakes, added to the top of cereal, or popped into lemonade. For the best results, collect the blossoms just after the dew has dried on the day you plan to use them, choosing ones that are flawless and fully open.

1¼ cups cold water

1 packet unflavored gelatin granules

¾ cup boiling water

1 pound extra-fine granulated sugar

Large bowl of sweet violet flowers (approx. 6 cups)

Tweezers

Small paintbrush

Wax paper

1. Pour ¼ cup of the cold water into a heat-proof large (16-ounce) glass measuring cup. Sprinkle the gelatin granules over the water and let it stand for 2 minutes.

2. Add the boiling water to the mixture and stir until the gelatin dissolves. Then pour in the remaining cup of cold water and stir until the mixture reaches room temperature.

3. Pour the sugar into a bowl.

4. One at a time, hold each flower by the stem with the tweezers and use the paintbrush to lightly dab gelatin onto both sides of it. Don't use too much gelatin or the sugar will lump. Drop the coated flower into the sugar and sprinkle more sugar on all its surfaces. Set the sugared flower on wax paper.

5. Leave the candied flowers on the wax paper, turning them several times, until they are completely dry. Then store the flowers in a tin lined with wax paper, but use them as soon as possible.

Violets

In ancient times and modern days, and in the East and the West, the violet has always been a favorite flower. The Persians and the Romans used it to make wine. It is my absolute favorite wildflower, with its tiny, delicate lavender-blue blossoms and heart-shaped leaves. Despite appearances, it is a very strong plant, one that is quick to spread. I weed violets out where they are challenging other flowering plants and leave them mostly between the stones in the walkway and as a ground cover under larger bushes.

Violets are a great source of vitamins A and C. You can use the flower heads to make a subtle but wonderful tea by putting a cup of the blossoms in a teapot and pouring boiling water over them (never boil the flower heads themselves). Let the tea steep for several minutes before drinking it. The heart-shaped leaves are edible, too. Fry them until browned and then squeeze lemon juice on them.

Cattails

Cattails (*Typha latifolia* and *angustifolia*) have several parts that are edible: the early shoots, the immature green flower heads, and the pollen, which can be harvested from the mature flower head.

Early in spring you can pick the shoots, which have a flat leaf surface similar to many other water-loving reeds. Remove the tough outer swordlike leaves and eat the plant's tender center. It tastes much like zucchini and is full of vitamin C, potassium, and beta-carotene. You can serve it raw or cooked. The immature green flower head, which tastes like corn on the cob, should be cooked. The pollen from the mature flowers is a high-energy food source (like bee pollen) and can be added to flour to produce nutritious, bright yellow baked goods.

Finding Cattails

Cattails grow near marshes and ditches and other places you might find still, shallow water. They also thrive along the edges of lakes and ponds. When used for decoration in a vase, they need to be sprayed with a fixative to prevent them from bursting open and spreading their powdery seeds.

Common Milkweed

The common milkweed plant has many edible parts and is often found growing in meadows and in vacant lots. Milkweed shoots can be harvested in early spring and will have a second sprouting if cut back.

This plant can be used decoratively as well. It has lovely silky seed clusters that can be sprayed with a fixative to prevent them from blowing around. When the buds finally open, the flowers are a light red to purple color.

These three grapevine wreaths adorned with dried milkweed pods were created by floral and garden designer Pamela Hardcastle.

Preparing Milkweed

To prepare the sprouts and young pods of the milkweed plant (*Asclepias syriaca*), drop them into boiling water and boil for seven minutes to eliminate any bitterness from the milky sap that runs through the plant. Once prepared, the taste of milkweed is very fresh and subtle. The earliest shoots are similar in flavor to asparagus and can be simply steamed with butter. The buds are like broccoli and can be enjoyed in similar ways. They should be picked while still green, before the flower blooms and becomes pink in color.

Wild Onion

Wild onion (*Allium* spp.) is an early spring treat that looks similar to chives and grows in masses in open fields. It is easy to dig up, especially since the soil tends to be moist at that time of year. Use the white parts only. Dice and fry them in a little olive oil, butter, or bacon fat, and they make a sweet, delicious addition to an omelet or fried potatoes.

Stinging Nettle

The stinging nettle (*Urtica dioica*) may seem off-putting with its irritating tiny hairs on its stem and the undersides of its leaves, but if you wear gloves to harvest the young and tender greens and use metal tongs while cleaning them, they're well worth the effort. And once you chop, crush, or cook it, the plant's stinging hairs are disabled. Highly nutritious, stinging nettle tastes similar to spinach and is a good choice for flavoring soups, pestos, or polenta.

Garlic Mustard

Garlic mustard (*Alliaria petiolata*) is an invasive weed and can be found almost everywhere, even in home flower beds. It is a highly nutritious green, particularly when young. The plant has a garlicky flavor and can be eaten raw, including the small white flowers. The roots make a good horseradish substitute, and the leaves can be used as a substitute for basil in pesto recipes.

Hickory Nuts

These nuts make a tasty snack. They ripen from September through October and are delicious in baked goods. In particular, those from the shagbark hickory (*Carya ovata*) are reliably tasty and easy to identify. Be prepared to work for the nuts, though; the shells are hard and thick, which can make them difficult to crack.

Acorns

To prepare these tree nuts, shell them and then boil them for two hours, changing the water each time it discolors to take out the bitter tannins. Eventually the water will no longer turn dark. Dry the kernels in the oven at 200°F for approximately 20 minutes, during which time they will turn a rich brown and smell fantastic. The baked nuts can be eaten as is or ground up and added to bread recipes, pancakes, or muffins.

Staghorn Sumac

Different species of staghorn sumac (*Rhus typhina*) grow throughout North America along roadsides, in open fields, and on the dry banks of streams, lakes, and rivers. Harvest the berries in July and August (some years they may even thrive into early October) by simply snapping or clipping the heads off. The darker berries are considered the best but the pink ones are delicious, too.

For a tart, refreshing drink, put five heads in a pitcher and pour cold water over them. Break up the berries with a wooden spoon or clean hands. Drain the liquid through cheesecloth and use it to make lemonade or tea. This same sumac juice can also be used to boil elderberries and other fruits when making jam to lend it a tart flavor.

Common Elderberries

The common elderberry bush (*Sambucus* spp.) is beautiful when it first blooms in spring with its giant saucer-sized white flower heads, which turn into the small clusters of wine-colored berries later in the summer. Elderberries are full of vitamin C and delicious for making wine, sparkling wine, pies, and jelly. You have to pick the berries early, though, or the birds will beat you to them. The flower heads make wonderful fritters or pancakes.

Making Elderberry Flower "Pancakes"

Pick the complete elderberry flower head, including a short portion of the stem to hold it by. Wash and drain it. Heat a couple tablespoons each of butter and oil in a heavy saucepan over medium heat. Then turn the flower upside down and dip it into pancake batter. Carefully lower the battered flower into the hot fat and fry it until light brown. Drain the flower pancake on a paper towel, sprinkle it with powdered sugar, and serve.

Juniper Berries

Juniper berries are beautiful to look at, but they also can be crushed and made into a tea rich in vitamin C. Native Americans traditionally used these berries to cure coughs, fevers, and tooth-aches. Juniper berries are ready to harvest in the fall, but like elderberries, they're popular with the birds, so you'll need to pick them early in the season. Because some juniper species are toxic, it's important to consult with an expert and correctly identify what you are harvesting.

Edible Estates

FRITZ HAEG IS AN ARTIST who isn't afraid to experiment. A case in point is his concept for creating "edible estates" by converting suburban lawns into lush gardens. In contrast to manicured lawns, which encourage isolation and perpetuate the consumption of precious fuel, edible gardens can connect us to our neighbors and make us more knowledgeable about and in tune with the cycles of nature as well as the process of food production. The aim is to grow fruits, nuts, vegetables, herbs, mushrooms, and other useful plants in a diverse and high-yield system that is largely self-maintained.

Haeg's initial Edible Estate project was funded by the Salina Art Center in Kansas, an organization with complementary interests in native plant species, prairie agriculture, and soil conservation. In July 2005, under Haeg's direction, a dedicated team of volunteer landscapers and gardeners installed the first Edible Estate in the front yard of Priti and Stan Cox's Salina home. The idea then spread to California and on to suburban New York. The endeavor continues, with additional gardens being installed and with Haeg conducting lectures on the project countrywide. He even offers guidelines online for people interested in attempting to create their own Edible Estates.

ECO TIP

The word "locavore" is a recent addition to Webster's dictionary and means a person who eats food grown or produced within a 100-mile radius. Canning and freezing are two means of preserving local summer crops for a supply that will last through the winter months.

The first Edible Estates project in Salina, Kansas, began with a suburban front lawn (top), from which the grass was removed (center) and replaced with a diverse food garden (bottom).

CHAPTER SEVEN

Holiday and Seasonal Decorations

WHEN IT COMES TO DECORATING FOR HOLIDAYS or parties, using natural elements can be exciting. Instead of going to the flower shop or craft store for supplies, simply go outside and scope around your yard, or take a trip to the woods. The materials will be fresh, free, and reflective of the season. Be creative and try combinations of different items, such as filling a hollowed-out log with bright maple leaves for a table centerpiece, or placing the leaves under a glass plate. Experiment with tying broken twigs and irises or other flowers together with a ribbon and setting the bouquet in a charming vase. Or top a large piece of bark with polished apples. The combinations are endless and fun. In this chapter, you'll find many creative and festive applications of natural materials for all four seasons.

Spring Table Designs

IN THE SPRING, THERE ARE SO MANY NATURAL WOODLAND ELEMENTS you can use to brighten up the tables and other spaces in your home. Early blooms such as tulips and daffodils can be gathered for bouquets. In addition, branches from many flowering trees and bushes can be forced, allowing you to enjoy them even before spring arrives.

BELOW
A twig goose overlooks a grapevine wreath that doubles as a basket. Tucked into the basket are a few large off-white goose eggs. Quince buds, mushrooms, moss, tulips, and daffodils arranged in a bark-covered vase complete this spring woodland display.

LEFT
An unusual spring bouquet features the exotic early buds of garden rhubarb and leaves the stalks available for making pies and jams.

Natural Egg Dyes

When dying eggs, naturalist Ivy Cote Fairbrother likes to use cooked beets, which she processes in a juicer. The resulting air bubbles give the dyed shells a mottled look. She also recommends blueberry juice and black tea as other sources to achieving variations in tone. Ivy recommends adding natural dyes and a teaspoon of vinegar (to speed the dying process) right to the pan of boiling eggs. When you're satisfied with the color, you can remove the eggs and set them back in the egg carton to dry. Or you can crush berries in a small cup, add a dash of white vinegar, and then paint the mixture directly onto the hard-cooked eggs.

There are many natural elements you can use to make dye, and the more concentrated the amount you use, the darker the color will be. Both fresh and frozen produce will work. Here is a list of some of the natural dye colors you can produce and the substances that will yield them.

For blue and lavender. Use wild grapes, wild raspberries, blueberries, or juniper berries.

For brown. Use boiled instant coffee or black walnut shells.

For green. Use boiled burdock leaves or knotweed leaves.

For yellow. Use lemon peels, daisy seed heads, or black-eyed Susan leaves.

For orange. Use bittersweet berries.

For purple. Use pokeweed berries.

For red. Use boiled red onion skins (use lots of them), cooked beets, or winterberries.

For pink. Use a small amount of cooked beets, cranberries, or cranberry juice.

For gray or black. Use black tea.

ABOVE
A glass garden table is set with chartreuse leaf-shaped dishes and small individual nests made from willow branches. Eggs dyed with blueberries and beets fill a grapevine basket adorned with pussy willows.

Spring Buds

Pussy willows are one of the very first signs of spring, with the buds that formed the previous fall opening to reveal the plants' fuzzy gray knobs. Simply cut them and bring them indoors. You don't even need to water them.

Forsythia, dogwood, and apple and cherry blossoms can also be cut in early spring and forced in water (be sure to change the water after the first week). They tend to bloom indoors within two weeks.

BELOW
Artist Mimi Krysiak arranged long-stemmed pussy willows across the ceiling beams of her summer porch to add a seasonal atmosphere to outdoor dining.

Propagation

Propagation is an inexpensive way to add selected plants to your own landscape. Pussy willows, forsythia, spirea, and honeysuckle are the easiest to propagate from a young branch. Take a cutting while the plant is still dormant. It should be 12 to 15 inches long to ensure it contains wood growth from the previous year, and it should contain at least two nodes (where the leaf bud attaches to the stem). Cut the branch about 2 inches below the bottom node. Fill a 6-inch-diameter garden pot with potting soil. Then dip the branch end in a rooting powder, insert it into the soil, and cover the branch with a plastic bag to simulate greenhouse conditions. Check weekly for roots, and once they have formed, remove the bag. Water the branch as needed and plant it outdoors as soon as the soil warms.

Seasonal Crowns

OIL PAINTER AND DESIGNER ANNE FREDERICKS is greatly influenced by her surroundings. Her home is set amid woods, fields, and wetlands, all of which yield a bounty of natural materials for crafting. She has drawers filled with all sorts of finds, including acorns, cones, insects, stones, and tortoise shells. In honor of the different seasons, Anne created four distinctive crowns using bits and pieces from her collection. Each was constructed on a small wire armature to which she hot-glued or wired the various elements.

CLOCKWISE FROM TOP LEFT
The spring crown is made from birds' nests filled with eggs from her neighbor's French pullets and sprays of apple blossoms.

For a summer crown, Anne used green moss, grass, garden-fresh strawberries, pink cosmos, pansies, roses, and lavender flowers. Butterflies, moths, and dragonflies suspended on thin wire hover over the arrangement.

This autumn crown primarily reflects the work of hornets. The base is a large papery nest, which she topped with honeycomb, wasp galls, elderberries, and flowers.

Winter's bounty covers this crown with sprays of white pine and spruce, rows of pinecones, kousa dogwood fruits, small hemlock cones, and berries.

A Woodland Summer Luncheon

A WOODLAND LUNCHEON held on a warm summer day at the Race Brook Lodge, in the heart of the Berkshires, provided guests the opportunity to honor and celebrate the beauty and abundance of nature in fashion, food, and interior design. A large, creatively recycled barn, designed by David Rothstein and set back in the woods, was the perfect environment for the nature lovers to gather. The atmosphere was relaxed and cool — perfect for sharing a menu of fresh fruits and vegetables, beech mushrooms, olive oil and truffle vinegar, fresh mozzarella, basil with garden tomatoes, and homemade sumac lemonade.

LEFT
A free-form wooden bowl holds a colorful array of garden vegetables and greens brought to the woodland luncheon by Allegra Graham.

BELOW
The Prosecco was chilled in a vintage wooden cooler filled with ice and topped with pinecones, and it was served with a garnish of elderberries.

ABOVE
I styled this summer spread for the luncheon by covering a porch table with a burlap cloth and added a centerpiece of fruit arranged in a hollowed-out log.

Dirty Little Tramp Martini

A seasonal drink created by Daniel Osman at the Dream Away Lodge in Becket, Massachusetts, features a creative combination: local Berkshire Ice Glen vodka and pickled spring ramps.

To make, swish a whisper of vermouth around a chilled martini glass. Pour a shot of Berkshire Ice Glen vodka into a cocktail shaker with crushed ice and a splash of pickled ramp juice (see Sarah Dibben's Pickled Ramps and Fiddleheads on page 116). Shake. Place one pickled ramp in the martini glass and pour the vodka over it.

ABOVE AND AT TOP
Luncheon guest Susan Schwartz adorned the hat she wore to the woodland luncheon with a small gourd, a pinecone, a feather, and bits of dried corn husks. Her great-uncle Frank designed her necklace, using peach and apricot pits he carved and then strung together with baling wire, metal clasps, and odds and ends found in his workshop.

RIGHT
Janet Cooper embellished a belt with dried flowers.

CLOCKWISE FROM TOP LEFT
Luncheon guest Vicci Recckio designed this party disguise by hot-gluing woodsy objects, such as miniature pinecones, sunflower seeds, mushrooms, acorns, and poppy pods, to a papier-mâché mask. A wisp of reed grass gives it a featherlike flair.

Vicci wears a Victorian-style hat I designed using seed flowers from the tree-of-heaven (Chinese sumac), moss, lichen, pinecones, and curls of bark.

A mink hat worn by Lisa Vollmer serves as a reminder of the fauna existing in the wild. The top is embellished with a fern, moss, and acorns.

Autumn Woodland Decorations

AUTUMN IS A TIME OF VIBRANT COLORS spawned by cooler temperatures that bring a sense of pending winter and begin to draw us indoors. Vegetable gardens offer up their late harvests, seedpods send seeds across the meadows, and trees shed their leaves. All around us is a virtual supermarket of natural materials to gather and use for eco-chic decor.

OPPOSITE, TOP TO BOTTOM
Dahlias and bittersweet berries are a complementary blend of offerings from late summer and the beginnings of fall.

I created this autumn table display with bright yellow dishes set on placemats fashioned from a scattering of colored maple and oak leaves. For a centerpiece, I filled a hollowed-out section of log with bittersweet and accented it with wild mushrooms, lime-colored black walnuts (the nuts are green before they turn black), and hickory nuts, as well as apples, garlic heads, and kohlrabi.

THIS PAGE, CLOCKWISE FROM TOP LEFT
Preserving leaves is an enjoyable project for both adults and children. Here is a sample of artwork my grandchildren and I did together. Coated with an acrylic sealer, mounted leaves and woodland bits will last a long time.

A wonderful combination of fall hues and textures are used to create this fall wreath designed by Barbara Bockbrader. In the mix are pinecones, seedpods, dried hydrangea petals, and poppy seedpods sprayed gold.

Wreaths made with reed grass, fern seedpods, and mullein leaves.

Colored Leaf Garland

Designed by Marlene Hurley Marshall

The technique for making this colorful door surround can also be used to create a bright Thanksgiving table runner. And if you set the table with glass plates, you'll be able to see the leaves beneath them. To make a garland or runner, you'll need to collect good leaf specimens in early autumn and dry them between newspaper sheets or magazines for a few days to keep them flat. Do not place leaves on top of each other because they will not dry properly and might mold.

Measuring tape

Scissors

10 yards burlap (5½ inches wide)

Wax paper or parchment paper

Paintbrush

Tacky glue

Fall leaves, dried and flattened

Hammer

Small finishing nails

1. Measure around your door frame and cut the burlap to length, leaving a little extra on each end for mounting it.

2. Cover your work surface with wax paper or parchment paper.

3. Use the paintbrush to apply a thin layer of tacky glue over a one-foot section of the burlap.

4. Press leaves onto the glued section. Then cover them with another piece of wax paper and gently place a magazine or book on top of it to press the leaves evenly into the glue and keep them flat.

5. Finish the garland a foot at a time, allowing the glue to dry thoroughly before removing the paper.

6. Use the finishing nails to tack the garland around the door frame. If it's an area that is exposed to high winds, you may want to use a staple gun to hold it more securely.

Autumn Leaf Bouquet

Fall leaves gathered early in the season are dazzling displayed in a red glass vase. Another fun way to show off fall leaves is to plunge them into a large clear glass vase filled with water.

A burlap runner covered with leaves trims a door frame with the vibrant colors of autumn. Here, the wind has also deposited a carpet of leaves at the threshold.

Fall Flora

Pamela **Hardcastle is an avid collector** of natural elements and has incorporated them in her interior designs, as well as in her fabulous gardens, for more than 15 years. She is best known for the creative ways she uses flora, such as tying full tree branches to columns, transforming bark into vessels for fruits or flowers, and turning live bushes into unique fences. "I love the untamed energy and rhythm of the woods," says Pamela. "Nature does not make mistakes with proportion and is therefore a perfect teacher."

Pamela's simple composition of autumn squash and large dried shelf mushrooms beautifully decks a fireplace mantle.

A large, delicate wreath of fern seedpods fashioned by Pamela hangs on this inn entrance door.

A simple application of seedpods and natural twine on a dining room door is subtle yet dramatic. Rolled bark accents the top of the door frame.

A Fall Wedding

The Normandy-style barn at Gedney Farm in New Marlborough, Massachusetts, is a striking setting to hold a wedding celebration. Here, Pamela Hardcastle creates woodland atmospheres with simple and captivating natural materials perfect for a November reception.

CLOCKWISE FROM TOP RIGHT
The wedding guests' tables are set with bark cradles topped with bright yellow quince, orange persimmons, and blue-green squash.

The head table, covered with rust-colored silk cloths and earthy burlap underskirts, is adorned with long dark cradles of bark filled with deep red pomegranates and amaryllis flowers. Votive candles cast soft light around the room.

A tall beech tree branch placed in an ornate urn decorates the barn entrance. A large piece of coarse tree bark and green squashes in a dry brush nest complete the scene.

Holiday Decorations

THE HOLIDAY SEASON IS A WONDERFUL TIME to bring nature indoors. Natural elements are easy to come by and a lot less expensive than store-bought decorations. You can create interesting garlands with fruit, pinecones, vines, and berries and use woodland elements to embellish green balsam wreaths and holiday trees.

THIS PAGE, BELOW LEFT
A square wreath made of dried magnolia leaves hangs on a painted country door.

THIS PAGE, BELOW RIGHT
This entranceway table is topped with amaryllis bulbs and small fern-seed-covered garden pots stuffed with evergreens to create a festive display of green and white holiday hues.

OPPOSITE, CLOCKWISE FROM TOP LEFT
This grand holiday table display, designed by Pamela Hardcastle, uses a large ball covered with piñon pinecones and trimmed with evergreen as the central focus.

Woodland style dressed to the hilt in this creative holiday window display at Bergdorf Goodman's department store.

Branches from the deciduous tree-of-heaven, lightly coated with silver paint and then dusted with gold powder, rest on two vintage mercury glass vases to create a winter environment on this fireplace mantle.

Aromatic Fire Pinecones

Place pinecones on a sheet of parchment paper in one-layer rows, a half inch apart from each other. Bake them at 200°F for about 20 minutes. Cool the cones completely and then place them in an airtight plastic container or plastic bag. Add about six drops of essential oil, such as balsam or clove, and shake the bag to distribute the oil. Seal the cones in the bag for a few weeks. When you're ready to use them, place a cone or two in a fireplace with the fire logs. Once the fire is lit, a holiday aroma will waft through your rooms.

CLOCKWISE FROM TOP LEFT
Crafter Joan Sussman designed this garland by wrapping fishing line around the tops of individual pinecones. The garland was created in two sections to make it manageable as a sizable string of cones is surprisingly heavy.

This fireplace mantle is decorated with evergreens, an urn filled with pinecones, and a large piñon pinecone ball designed by Pamela Hardcastle.

A rustic pine box filled with evergreen boughs and draped with a pinecone garland adds seasonal flair to a country porch.

Mullein Florets

Mullein is a biennial plant that grows in sunny, dry, gravelly soil. The leaf florets appear the first year and grow in a large clump of gray-green fuzzy leaves that are as large as feet. During its second year, mullein sends up a stout flower stem that can grow 10 feet tall or more.

To harvest mullein leaf florets, dig them up with a trowel. Be sure to salvage as much as you can of the plant surrounding the center floret as well as the important taproot for attaching wire to.

Magical Miniature Worlds

NEW YORK BOTANICAL GARDEN'S ANNUAL HOLIDAY TRAIN SHOW, featuring miniature replicas of landmark buildings and bridges in the greater New York area, is truly a sight to behold. The creator of this fairyland is award-winning artist and landscape architect Paul Busse. As the owner of Applied Imagination of Alexandria, Kentucky, Paul designs extraordinary miniature worlds at botanical gardens and public spaces around the country, using historic buildings as models. He started his career in the 1980s, creatively pairing items of different scale to create magical illusions. For example, he might place a miniature Japanese maple next to a miniature building to achieve the look of a sprawling full-sized tree.

The detail work on Paul's train-show showpieces is breathtaking: window mullions made from tiny sticks, balconies exquisitely constructed from curled grapevine, and stair rails shaped from twisted twigs. The entire historic village is landscaped with moss, ferns, flowering plants, and stones, and each building is lit from within. And with pathways you can follow under the bridges, trains and trolleys scooting along the rails, and flowing waterfalls, the installation offers a magical experience for children of all ages.

TOP TO BOTTOM
A miniature of the New York Public Library is complete with lions lounging on the grand steps and statues made of straw stationed above the arched entrances.

Pinecone towers top Paul Busse's Ellis Island Immigration Station (circa 1900). The piece is set up in the Haupt Conservatory in the Bronx and is the first exhibit in the Holiday Train Show.

Made with strips of bark, Paul Busse's Rockefeller Center building is boldly stationed in the middle of his miniature city.

CLOCKWISE FROM TOP LEFT
This wonderful wooden recreation of the Brooklyn Bridge, which spans the walkway at New York Botanical Garden, is the work of artist and landscape architect Paul Busse.

With railings made from grapevine tendrils, this staircase depicts the front of a classic brownstone.

This charming vintage New York cottage, set in a miniature landscape, features an acorn roof and twig porch columns.

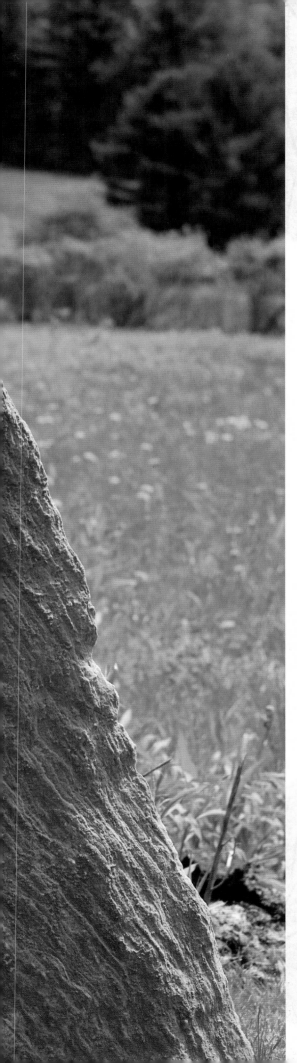

CHAPTER EIGHT

Stone and Faux Bois

STONE IS A NATURAL SOLID FORMATION of earthy or mineral materials. Because it is so strong and durable, it has been a favored building material since ancient Egyptian times. Remarkably, some stone structures built as long as 5,000 years ago are still standing.

Stone has long been a favored medium in art as well. Not only has the raw material itself inspired amazing sculptures and carvings, but stone has inspired other forms of art. Faux bois (a French phrase that means "false wood") and ferrocement faux bois, for example, are art techniques that use cement-based media to fabricate objects that look as if they are made of wood. (Ferrocement faux bois objects have an iron or steel understructure.)

A naturally pierced stone dragged by Peter Thorne from the woods on one of his many walks now stands tall in his garden.

Balancing Rocks

STACKING STONES INTO MOUNDS TO CREATE A MEMORIAL OR LAND-MARK is an art form that dates back thousands of years and across many cultures, including the Alaskan Inuit and Korean monks. These mounds, known as cairns, can be found in alpine or mountainous regions as well as in barren deserts or on beaches. They are traditionally built for a variety of reasons. They might indicate a burial site or a summit, mark a direction, or commemorate an event. In medieval times, they often served as boundary markers. Cairns can range in size and shape from small piles of stones to enormous sculptures that are true feats of engineering. Cairns are created using only rocks. There are no supports or adhesives. Rather, the sculptures rely on the physics of stacks, arches, spires, and natural counterbalances. Today, the practice of rock balancing is more than an art form. It's also a hobby and a tool of meditation.

BELOW LEFT
A round garden pot created from cemented river rocks is filled with a fern plant at Madison Art and Antiques in Hudson, New York.

BELOW RIGHT
Artist Susan Oken's faux bois stand is the perfect prop for serving up a chocolate cake decorated with fresh flowers.

ABOVE
Artist Peter Thorne balanced this large rock atop stacked stones in the middle of his garden.

Faux Bois

MEXICAN SCULPTOR DIONICIO RODRIGUEZ is credited with popularizing faux bois in the United States when he worked in San Antonio, Texas, in the early 1900s. Rodriguez spoke no English and was extremely protective of his techniques, sharing information about his craft only with his nephew Maximo Cortès, who later instructed his son, Carlos Cortès. Carlos continues the family tradition in San Antonio today.

Rodriguez worked from the early 1920s to around 1940 and left a legacy of work thought to have been commissioned by Charles Baumberger, the owner of San Antonio Portland Cement Company (now Alamo Cement Company). One such creation is a large gate into the Chinese Tea Garden in Brackenridge Park, San Antonio. Also in the park is his charming log bridge in the faux bois tradition that is still in remarkably good condition today.

BELOW
A rare vintage faux bois bench, circa 1920 from Paris, France, sits beside Susan Oken's swimming pool in the middle of her garden on Martha's Vineyard.

ABOVE
A faux bois table, also circa 1920 from Paris, is topped with a contemporary faux bois planter filled with ferns and moss.

Mastering Faux Bois

Donald Tucker, a talented contemporary faux bois artist, and a friend of Carlos Cortès, studied the works of Dionicio Rodriguez and then essentially taught himself the art through determination and a lot of trial and error. Knowing that there is no bible or master manual on faux bois, Tucker has decided to school a few students in the history and technique of this lost art form.

He describes the process of creating this faux bois table above as complex and technically challenging, explaining that it involves first building a steel framework that sculptors call an armature, then securing and forming a metal mesh to it. The frame is then built up with multiple layers of concrete, mortar, and, oftentimes, pure cement paste. Next, Tucker roughs up the surface with a wooden rasp and uses an old butter knife to carve wood and bark textures into the wet concrete just as it reaches a certain stage of drying. The carvings are so realistic that they can fool the eye even when you're standing just inches away. Tucker even adds rusted bolts that appear to hold the structure together.

ABOVE
Three contemporary faux bois stools topped with moss seat cushions provide a quiet spot to chat under a tree in artist Susan Oken's yard.

BELOW LEFT
Maidenhead ferns fill a matching pair of contemporary faux bois planters from Oken's collection.

BELOW RIGHT
Rocks collected by artist Oken are displayed on a faux bois table.

Cement Leaves

Designed by David Boag

David Boag has many creative interests. A cheesemaker by profession, he is also an avid gardener, cook, and photographer. Using hosta plants from his backyard garden, he creates beautiful decorative cement leaves. His technique works well with other types of leaves, too, provided they have a strong vein structure. Most of the other materials you need for this project, including the plastic utility tub and play sand (which comes in large bags), can be purchased at a hardware or lumber store.

Large plastic utility tub

Play sand

Good-sized leaves with
  large veins

Trowel

Mortar mix (half Portland
  cement and half sand)

Large plastic bucket

Water

Large mixing stick

Cement colorant (optional)

Heavy plastic gloves

Sandpaper

1. Fill the utility tub with several inches of play sand (the sand can be reused).

2. Place the leaves facedown on the sand.

3. Place a couple trowelfuls of mortar mix in the bucket. Add enough water, stirring with a sturdy stick, to achieve a mudlike consistency. (If you are making colored leaves, add the cement colorant to the mortar mix before adding water.)

4. Spoon a few dollops of the mixture onto each leaf. With gloved hands, carefully spread the mortar onto the back of each leaf, pressing down lightly to get rid of any air pockets. The mortar should be about 1½ inches thick on the middle of the leaf and thin out to about 1 inch at the edges of the leaf.

5. Let the cement leaves cure undisturbed for two or more days (it can take longer if the temperature is low or the humidity is high). Cover the project if you are leaving it outdoors.

6. When the cement is completely cured, peel off the leaves. Use sandpaper to smooth any rough edges, if desired.

Recommended Reading

Creasy, Rosalind. *The Complete Book of Edible Landscaping.* San Francisco: Sierra Club Books, 1982.

Dunnett, Nigel, and Nöel Kingsbury. *Planting Green Roofs and Living Walls.* Portland, OR: Timber Press, 2004.

Durston, Diane. *Wabi Sabi: The Art of Everyday Life.* North Adams, MA: Storey Publishing, 2006.

Earth Pledge. *Green Roofs: Ecological Design and Construction.* Atglen, PA: Schiffer Publishing, 2004.

Johnson, Cathy. *The Wild Foods Cookbook.* Brattleboro, VT: Stephen Greene Press, 1989.

Kingsbury, Nöel. *Natural Garden Style: Gardening Inspired by Nature.* London: Merrell, 2009.

McEvoy, Marian. *Glue Gun Décor: How to Dress Up Your Home — from Pillows and Curtains to Sofas and Lampshades.* New York: Stewart, Tabori and Chang, 2005.

Reames, Richard. *Arborsculpture: Solutions for a Small Planet.* Williams, OR: Arborsmith Studios, 2005.

Rocca, Alessandro. *Natural Architecture.* New York: Princeton Architectural Press, 2007.

Thayer, Sam. *The Forager's Harvest.* Self-published, 2006.

Contributing Artists

MARLENE HURLEY MARSHALL
Author/Artist
marleneveronica@hotmail.com
www.marlenemarshallmosaics.com

Olena Bachinsky
Artist/Floral Designer
obachinsky@gmail.com

Patrick Blanc
Artist
Vertical Garden
info@murvegetalpatrickblanc.com
www.verticalgardenpatrickblanc.com

David Boag
Artist
davidrboag@aol.com

Anna Brahms
Artist/Dollmaker
aabrahms@verizon.net

Sara Burke
Artist/Wool Dyes
bluegrassdoll@verizon.net

Paul Busse
Landscape Architect
Applied Imagination
info@appliedimagination.biz
www.appliedimagination.biz

Len Campanale
Artist
52lencamp@comcast.net

Carole Clark
Artist
518-851-8987
www.caroleclark.net

Janet Cooper
Artist
413-229-8012
www.janetcooperdesigns.com

Ivy Cote Fairbrother
Artist
ivy@fairbrother.com

Jack DeMuth
Furniture Designer
978-201-1028
http://jackdemuth.com

Patrick Dougherty
Sculptor
Business inquiries: *branchwork@ earthlink.net*
Other inquiries: *stickwork@earthlink. net*
www.stickwork.net

Erica Fielder
Eco-Artist
Bird Feeder Hat project
erica@ericafielder-ecoartist.com
www.ericafielder-ecoartist.com
www.birdfeederhat.org

Anne Fredericks
Artist
http://annefredericks.com
www.mermaiddesignllc.com

Ann Getsinger
Artist
413-229-2119
www.anngetsinger.com
See Ann Getsinger's paintings at:
Dowling Walsh Gallery
357 Main Street
Rockland, ME 04841
www.dowlingwalsh.com

James Gottlieb
Artist
gottliebgallery@aol.com

Robin Greeson
Artist
mcgory@bcn.net

Ellen Grenadier
Artist
413-528-9973
www.grenadierpottery.com

Pamela Reed Hardcastle
Floral and Garden Designer
413-229-8812
www.pamelahardcastle.com

Susie Hardcastle
Artist
susiehardcastle@gmail.com

Linda Horn
Artist/Naturalist
lindabhorn@yahoo.com

Kevin Inkawhich
Sculptor
kevin_ink@mac.com

Mimi Krysiak
Artist
krysiak@verizon.net

Alex Malarkey
Fence Designer
Great Barrington, MA 01230

John Manikowski
Artist
413-229-2905
www.johnmanikowski.com

Joan Meakin
Artist
jmeakin@netzero.net

Michael Melle
Sculptor
michael@scarecrowgarden.com
www.scarecrowgarden.com

Mariette Moon
Floral Designer
mariotter428@verizon.net

Tyler Moore
Sculptor
Tyla_mo@yahoo.com

Nick Nickerson
Artist
jberne@taconic.net
www.NickNick.com

Nic Osborn and Robin Sweeney
Artists
robinsweeney@earthlink.net

Gail Peachin
Artist
Fern Antique Shop
610½ Warren Street
Hudson, NY 12534

José Pimentel
Artist
josefranklin@yahoo.com

Richard Reames
Arborsmith
richard@arborsmith.com
www.arborsmith.com

Joan Sussman
Artist
joanpsussman@msn.com

Peter Thorne
Furniture Designer
pgthorne@hotmail.com

Sarah Thorne
Interior Designer
sarahkthorne@gmail.com

Sabine Vollmer von Falken
Photographer
413-298-4933
www.sabinephotoart.com

Wenonah Webster
Floral and Garden Designer
518-755-9621
www.wenonahwebster.com

Tom Zetterstrom
Activist/Photographer
http://tomzetterstrom.com
www.elmwatch.org

Other Contributors

The following businesses, nonprofit organizations, and people welcomed us in to photograph their collections, exhibits, wares, and products. We are grateful and honored to be able to feature them in this book.

Campo de' Fiori
Woodland Garden Shop
Barbara Bockbrader and Robin Norris
1815 North Main Street (Route 7)
Sheffield, MA 01257
413-528-1857
www.campodefiori.com

The Dream Away Lodge
Daniel Osman
1342 County Road
Becket, MA 01223
www.thedreamawaylodge.com

Gedney Farm
Leslie Miller and Brad Wagstaff
Route 57
34 Hartsville–New Marlboro Road
New Marlborough, MA 01230
800-286-3139
www.gedneyfarm.com

Hudson Home
356 Warren Street
Hudson, NY 12534
518-822-8120
www.hudson-home.com

Keystone
Jim Godman
746 Warren Street
Hudson, NY 12534
www.godmanskeystone.com

Lili and Loo
259 Warren Street
Hudson, NY 12534
www.liliandloo.com

Madison Art and Antiques
347 Warren Street
Hudson, NY 12534
413-297-5140

Moss Acres
David and Al Benner
866-438-6677
www.mossacres.com

The New York Botanical Garden
Bronx River Parkway at Fordham Road
Bronx, NY 10458-5126
718-817-8700
www.nybg.org

The Olana Partnership
5720 State Route 9G
Hudson, NY 12534
518-828-0135
www.olana.org

The Old Inn On The Green
Peter Platt, Chef/Owner
134 Hartsville Road
New Marlborough, MA 01230
413-299-7924
www.oldinn.com

Rustic Designs
Don McAulay Jr.
20 Maple Avenue
Erving, MA 01344
413-221-6173
www.customrusticfurniture.com

Stagecoach Tavern at Race Brook Lodge
Sara Dibben, Chef
864 South Undermountain Road
Sheffield, MA 01257
413-229-8585
www.stagecoachtavern.net

Strawberry Farm
Susan Schwartz
sschwartz01256@yahoo.com

Vince Mulford Antiques
419 Warren Street
Hudson, NY 12534
518-828-5489
www.vmulford.com

Wild Pantry
Bonnie Morris
912-225-1424
www.wildpantry.com

Resources

Columbia Pine Cones and Botanicals
888-470-6989
www.pinecones.com

Halcyon Yarn
800-341-0282
www.halcyonyarns.com
Glauber's salt for dyeing wool

Pinecones of the Northwest
800-613-1242
www.pineconesofthenorthwest.com

Winter Woods
800-541-4511
www.winterwoods.com
Forest naturals

Birch Forest
207-668-2163
www.birchbarkstore.com
Birch bark

Index

Page numbers in italics indicate photographs.

A

acorns, 47, 56–57, *56, 57*
  collecting & storing, 16, 56
  cooking with, 123
  decorating with, *51, 61,* 101
  jewelry of, 57, *57*
antlers, *33, 102*
arbors, 97, *97*
autumn decorations, 131, *131,* 136–41, *136, 137, 138, 140, 141*
autumn foraging, 14

B

Bachinsky, Olena, 23
bark, 19, 83, 100–105
  collecting & storing, 14, 16, 100
  decorating with, *66,* 104, *104, 141*
  figures of, *97*
  on frames, 41, *41,* 52–53, *52*
  in potpourri, 76, *76–77*
  types of, *13*
  See also birch bark
baskets, pine needle, 55, *55*
belts, *134*
benches, *42, 151*
Benner, Al and David, 60
birch bark, 100–103
  birdhouses, 100, *100, 102*
  birthday cake, 101, *101*
  canoes, 99, *99*
  curtains, 101, *101*
  decorating with, 102, *102, 103, 105*
birch logs & trees, *31, 43,* 98, *98*
  ceilings, 92, *93, 95*
  Heather Houses, *9*
  porches, 94–95, *94, 95*
bird feeders, 38–39, *38, 39,* 102, *103*
birdhouses, 100, *100, 102*
bird nests, 37, *37, 131*
bittersweet
  chairs of, *28, 31*
  nymphs, 20–21, *20, 21*
  table decorations, *136,* 137
Blanc, Patrick, 69, *69*
blooms, forcing, 14, 128, 130, *130*
Boag, David, 154
Brahms, Anna, 45, *45*
branches, 8, *22, 50, 141*

figures of, 22, *22*
forcing blooms on, 14
furniture of, 31–33, *31, 32, 33, 94*
houses of, *36*
nymphs of, 20–21, *20, 21*
wreaths of, 24
Brockbrader, Barbara, *137*
buildings
  Heather Houses, 8–9, *9*
  island woodland, 96–97, *96, 97*
  living roofs for, 68, *68*
  miniature worlds, 146–47, *146, 147*
  of saplings, 34–36, *34, 35, 36*
  tree house, 88–91, *88, 89, 91*
  vertical gardens on, 69, *69*
  of vines, *18–19*
  woodsy cottages, 92–93, *92, 93*
Burke, Sara, 79
Busse, Paul, 146–47, *146, 147*

C

cairns, 150
Campanale, Len, *102*
candleholders, *145*
canoes, birch bark, 99, *99*
cattails, 120, *120*
cedar, 26, *26, 57,* 89, *89*
ceilings, 92, *93, 95*
ceramic leaf designs, 70–71, *70, 71*
chairs
  deer antler, *33*
  hickory, *42*
  hoop-back, *31*
  living, *87*
  mortised branch, *94*
  of saplings, *33, 43,* 87, *87*
  of vines, *28, 29*
  whimsical, *73, 73*
chandeliers, *22, 102*
chicken of the woods, 110, *110*
Church, Frederic, 30
Clark, Carole, 105, *105,* 109
clothing, 20–21, *20, 21,* 45, *45*
Cooper, Janet, 20–21, *20, 21, 134*
cottages, woodsy, 92–93, *92, 93, 147*
crowns, seasonal, 131, *131*
curtains, *50,* 101, *101*

D

dandelions, 118, *118*
daylilies, 118, *118*
DeMuth, Jack, 31, *31*
Dibben, Sarah, 111, *111*

fiddlehead recipes, 116, *116*
  mushroom recipes, 112, *112, 113, 113*
  ramp recipes, 114, *115, 116*
  wild grape jelly, 117, *117*
dolls, 45, *45*
doors, *88, 89,* 138, *139, 140*
Dougherty, Patrick, *18–19,* 34–36, *34, 35, 36*
duck, bamboo, *43*
dyes, natural, 78–79, *78, 79,* 129, *129*

E

eggs, 37, 129, *129*
elderberry, common, 124, *124*
Erlandson, Axel, 86, *86, 87, 87*
evergreens, 8, *143, 144*

F

faeries, woodland, 45, *45*
Fairbrother, Ivy Cote, 129
faux bois, 149, 151–53, *151, 152, 153*
fences, 30, *30*
ferns, 16, 64–65, *65, 70, 71, 135, 140*
fiddleheads, 116, *116*
Fielder, Erica, 38–39, *38, 39*
figures
  dancing, *23*
  dolls, 45, *45*
  garden nymphs, 20–21, *20, 21*
  hay and stick, 22, *22*
  log and bark, *97*
  root people, 44, *44*
fireplace mantle, *140, 143, 144*
fixatives, 76
foraging, 11–14, *12, 13, 14*
forcing blooms, 14, 128, 130, *130*
frames
  mirror, *33, 51,* 52–53, *52*
  picture, 41, *41, 54,* 55, *55, 56, 56*
Fredericks, Anne, 102, *103,* 131, *131*
furniture
  of branches and twigs, 31–33, *31, 32, 33*
  campsite, 29, *29*
  of roots, 42, *42*
  of vines, 28–29, *28, 29, 31*
  See also chairs; tables

G

gardens
  edible, 125, *125*
  moss, 60, 62–63, *63*

roof, 68, *68*
  vertical, 69, *69*
  wildflower meadow, 80–81, *81*
garlands, 138, *139, 144*
garlic mustard, 122, *122*
Getsinger, Ann, *54,* 55
glues, 17
goose, of twigs, *128*
Gottlieb, James, *43*
grape jelly, 117, *117*
grapevines. *See* vines
grasses, 59, 80, 81, *81, 137*
greens, 59, 114, *115, 116,* 118, *118,* 122, *122*
Greeson, Robin, 57, *57*
Grenadier, Ellen, 70–71, *70, 71*

H

Hardcastle, Pamela, 140, *140, 141, 143, 144*
Hardcastle, Susie, 101, *101, 121*
hats, *48,* 72, *72*
  birdfeeder, 38–39, *38, 39*
  seasonal, 131, *131, 134, 135*
Heather Houses, 8–9, *9*
hemlock cones, 48, 56, *56*
Hen of the Woods, *108,* 109
hickory nuts, 123, *123*
holiday decorations, 127, 142–47, *142, 143, 144, 145, 146*
Horn, Linda, *72,* 81, *81*

I

Inkawhich, Kevin, 40, *40*
island woodland home, 96–97, *96, 97*

J

Japanese knotweed, 113, *113*
jewelry, 57, *57, 134*
juniper berries, 26, *26,* 124, *124*

K

kitchens, 89, *90,* 91, 92
knot handles, *88,* 89
Krysiak, Mimi, *22,* 73, *73, 130*

L

lamps, *31, 32, 102*
landscapes, miniature, 64–65, *65*
leaves, 59, 138, *138*
  cement, 154–55, *155*
  ceramic, 70–71, *70, 71*
  decorating with, *72, 73, 73*
  garland of, 138, *139*
  storing and preserving, 16, *137*

lichen, 14, 102, *103, 108*
locavore, 125
logs, 83, 92, *92*
  figures of, *97*
  planters of, *97*
  table decorations, *132, 133, 136*, 137, *141*
  See also birch logs & trees

M
Mankowski, John, *99*
maple sugaring, 117, *117*
Marshall, Marlene Hurley, 27, *27*, 66–67, *67*, 104, *104*, 138, *139*
martini, 133, *133*
masks, *135*
McAulay, Don, 94
Meakin, Joan, 44, *44*
medallion, pinecone, 49, *49*
Medusa, *43*
Melle, Michael, 22, *22*
milkweed, 121, *121, 140*
mirrors, *33, 51*, 52–53, *52*
mobiles, 40, *40*
Moon, Mariette, *57*
morels, 111, *111*, 112, *112*
moss, *9*, 59, 60–67, *60*
  collecting & storing, 14, 16
  decorating with, 61, *61*, 101, *101, 135*
  gardens, 60, 62–63, *63*
  tables covered with, 61, *61*
  in terrariums, 64–65, *65*
  types of, *13*, 62
  wreaths, 66–67, *66, 67*, 102, *103*
moth deterrents, *57*
mullein florets, *137*, 145, *145*
mushrooms
  decorating with, *54*, 55, 66
  edible, 108–12, *108, 110, 111, 112*

N
nature, reverence for, 8, 98, *99*
New York Botanical Garden, 146–47, *146, 147*
Nickerson, Nick, 41, *41*
nymphs, 20–21, *20, 21*

O
Oken, Susan, *36*, 96–97, *96, 97, 150, 151, 153*
Olana estate, 30, *30*
onions, wild, 122, *122*
Osborne, Nic, 88–91, *88, 89, 91*
Osman, Daniel, 133

P
papier-mâché, 38–39, *38, 39*
Peachin, Gail, *61, 66*, 101, *101*
piñon pinecones, *50, 143, 144*
pickles, 116, *116*, 133, *133*
picture frames, 41, *41, 54*, 55, *55, 56, 56*
Pimentel, José, 100
pinecones, 47, 48–54, *50*
  aromatic fire, 144
  collecting & storing, 14, 16
  decorating with, 8, *8*, 49, *49, 50*, 101, *144*
  on hats, *48*, 131, *135*
  on mirror frames, 52–53, *52*
  in potpourri, 76, *76–77*
  towers of, *146*
  on wreaths, 27, *27*, 48, *49*, 102, *103*, 137
pine needles, 24, 55, *55, 71*
planters, *50, 97*, 102, *103*
  faux bois, *151, 153*
  river rock, *150*
plants, 16, 64–65, *65*, 130
potpourri, 76, *76–77*
propagation, 130
puffballs, 110, *110*
pussy willows, 130, *130*

Q
Queen Anne's lace, *25*, 70–71, *78, 78*

R
railings, *89, 96*
ramps, 114–16, *114, 115, 116*, 133, *133*
Reames, Richard, 87
rocks, *148, 149*, 150, *150*
roofs, living, 68, *68*
roots, 19, 42–44
  fences of, 30, *30*
  furniture of, *32*, 42, *42*
  woodland figures of, 44, *44*

S
saplings, *97*
  buildings of, 34–36, *34, 35, 36*
  chairs of, *33, 43*, 87, *87*
Schwartz, Susan, 117, *134*
seedpods, 16, 47
  fern, *140*
  on frames, *51, 54*, 55, *55*
  milkweed, 121, *121, 140*
  on wreaths, 48, *49, 137*
spring decorations, 128–31, *128, 129, 130, 131*

spring foraging, 14
staghorn sumac, 123, *123*
staircase, *89, 92*, 93
starburst pattern, 8
stinging nettle, 122, *122*
stone, 14, *148*, 149, 150, *150*
stools, faux bois, *153*
summer decorations, 131, *131*, 132–35, *132, 133, 134, 135*
summer foraging, 14
Sussman, Joan, *144*
Sweeney, Robin, 41, *41*

T
table decorations
  for autumn, 136, *136*, 141, *141*
  for holidays, *142, 143*
  for spring, 128–29, *128, 129*
  for summer, *132, 133*
tables, *32*, 61, *61*
  campsite, 29, *29*
  faux bois, *151, 153*
terrariums, 16, 64–65, *65*
Thorne, Peter, 28, 29, *29, 148, 149, 150*
Thorne, Sarah, 48, *49*
tools, 12
tree house, 88–91, *88, 89, 91*
trees, 83–85, *84, 85, 91*, 98
tree sculpture, 86–87, *86, 87*
twigs, 8, *8, 9*, 19, 22, 37, *128*
  collecting & storing, 14, 16
  dancing figures of, *23*
  frames of, 41, *41*, 52–53, *52*
  furniture of, 31–33, *31, 32, 33*
  in potpourri, 76, *76–77*

V
vases, *50*, 104, *104*, 105, *105*
vines, 19, 23, 24–30
  collecting & storing, 14, 16, 24
  fences of, 30, *30*
  flowering, 26, *26*
  furniture of, 28–29, *28, 29, 31*, 61, *61*
  nymphs of, 20–21, *20, 21*
  wreaths of, 24–27, *24, 25, 26, 27*, 48, *49*, 121, *121*
violets, 73, *74*, 119, *119*

W
Webster, Wenonah, 64–65, *65, 145*
weddings, 141, *141*
wild edibles, 107–25
  foraging for, 12, 107
  greens, 114–16, *114, 115, 116*, 118, *118*, 122, *122*

mushrooms, 108–12, *108, 110, 111, 112*
  wildflowers, 118–19, *118, 119*
wildflowers, 14, 59, 74–81, *74*
  arrangements of, 73, *74*
  decorating with, *25*, 72, *72, 134*
  drying, 74
  edible, 118–19, *118, 119*
  meadow gardens, 80–81, *81*
  in potpourri, 76, *76–77*
willow, 24, 34–36, *34, 35, 36*
winter, 14, *14*
woodland materials
  cleaning, 15, *15*
  collecting, 11–14, *12, 13, 14*
  storing and preserving, 16, *16*
wool dyes, 78–79, *78, 79*
wreaths, 24–27, *24, 25, 26*, 142, *145*
  for autumn, *137*
  bark and lichen, 102, *103*
  of fern seedpods, *140*
  juniper berry, 26, *26*
  milkweed pods on, 121, *121*
  moss, 66–67, *66, 67*, 102, *103*
  pinecones on, 27, *27*, 48, *49*, 102, *103, 137*
  princess pine, 27, *27*

Z
Zetterstrom, Tom, *84, 85, 85*